SPACE AND SOCIETY 3

URBAN SYSTEMS

Andrew Kirby and David Lambert

LONGMAN

LONGMAN GROUP LIMITED
Longman House
Burnt Mill, Harlow, Essex CM20 2JE, England
and Associated Companies throughout the world.

First published 1984
ISBN 0 582 35357 2

Set in 10/11pt Baskerville, Linotron 202

*Printed in Singapore by
The Print House (Pte) Ltd*

Contents

Acknowledgements

We are grateful to the following for permission to reproduce copyright material:

Frances Pinter Publishers Ltd for extracts from *Urban Political Economy* by Kenneth Newton; Retail and Planning Associates and the author, R. L. Davies, for an extract from *Marketing Geography*.

We are grateful to the following for permission to reproduce photographs:

Aerofilms, page 76; Associated Press, page 80; Crown copyright, RAF Farnborough, page 75; Sefton Photo Library, page 77.

Preface

To the teacher

Aims

This series is designed for use within the sixth form as a back-up to the now familiar texts such as Tidswell's *Patterns and Process in Human Geography*, Bradford and Kent's *Human Geography* and Haggett's *Modern Synthesis*. We have designed the books as 'readers', that is, free-standing volumes that elaborate on particular topics, fleshing out the bare bones introduced within the textbook by presenting extracts from original sources and illustrative exercises. The latter are particularly important, as the emphasis throughout the series is upon the practical application of ideas, models and theories, rather than the abstract discussion of such deductive concepts. In this sense, the aim is to use the student's existing experiences of the 'real world' as a foundation for investigation, in order that these can be channelled into a systematic understanding of basic geographic principles.

Organisation

This book can be used in three ways. It is intended for use as a whole; in other words, the student should be able to use both the practical material and the original extracts in approaching a particular topic. In some instances, however, this may not be required. In such cases, it should be possible to use the practical examples alone, or if required, the published extracts as reference material.

Within each volume, a standard format is used. The authors' text is interspersed with secondary material, and at the end of each section there are questions, a check-list and notes which are designed to highlight the key issues that have been introduced. The latter are referred to throughout the text.

To the student

This book is one of a series of geography 'readers'. This means that
the aim of the series is not to provide a complete source of facts and
information for your sixth-form course; instead the intention is to
provide a firm grounding in some of the fundamental ideas within
the subject.

You should aim to read the volumes in the series as a back-up to
your course. If you have problems in understanding some sections,
discuss them with your teacher. There are, however, check-lists of
key issues at the end of each chapter which you should refer to, and
many of the ideas will become clearer as you work through the
examples.

1
The British urban system

1.1 Introduction

In the first two books of this series, we considered the two fundamental geographical concerns: regions and interaction. In this
volume, we will now begin to link these two concepts.

We have seen that all individuals possess an action space, that
is, a spatial area within which they go about their day-to-day business. In our study of interaction, we concentrated on the factors
that limit the action space – the frictions of distance. In this book,
we want to be a great deal more specific. We want to examine the
URBAN SYSTEM, the structure of towns and cities, and their
surrounding regions, which has evolved to both serve and contain
the many individual action spaces which together constitute the
British urban pattern.

We have called this book *Urban Systems*. However, we shall not
at first concentrate upon the factors that distinguish towns from
cities, or even urban from rural environments. Nor do we want to
concentrate upon any individual settlement; that topic will be
covered in Book 4 of the series, *The City*. The fundamental point we
wish to emphasise is that the urban system is ubiquitous. Except
for the lonely crofter, we are all components within an interlocking
collection of urban areas and their hinterlands. Even the most
rustic village is connected to this mesh; it will supply commuters
to neighbouring settlements and depend upon the latter for various
services like health care or shops. As we shall see, less than 5 per
cent of the British population can be thought of as being truly rural,
in the sense that it is outside this urban net.

1.2 The daily urban system

The essence of this view of urban areas is that it represents the day-
to-day movements of population; consequently it is termed a 'daily
urban system'. A more precise definition is provided by the geographers who have worked to understand British towns and cities
(Drewett, Goddard and Spence 1975. p. 524):

In searching for a functional definition of urban areas a central concept must be that of the urban field or daily urban system linking places of work and residential areas. Such systems define part of the social environment; for example, job opportunities for individuals, and of the economic environment; for example, potential employees . . . These definitions provide for areas which are basically employment cores and commuting hinterlands. The cores are made up of contiguous local authority areas with densities greater than 5 per acre or a total employment of over twenty thousand. The commuting hinterland is divided into two areas: first, a metropolitan ring area, defined as comprising local authority areas having more than 15 per cent of the economically active population commuting to the core. Second, an outer metropolitan ring area, defined as comprising all other contiguous local authorities having a more economically active population commuting to a particular core than to any other core. The core and metropolitan ring area defines the Standard Metropolitan Labour Area (SMLA) which normally has a total population of seventy thousand plus. The SMLA and the outer metropolitan ring area defines the Metropolitan Economic Labour Area (MELA) – the total urban system.

There are 126 MELAs in Britain. Together they contained population (and employment) in the following proportions in 1971 (1981 analysis has not yet taken place).

Table 1.1   *The distribution of population and employment within the SMLAs and MELAs in 1971*

Area	Population (%)	Employment (%)
Urban Cores (1)	47.4	58.6
Metropolitan rings (2)	31.9	22.9
SMLAs (1 + 2)	79.3	81.4
Outer metropolitan rings (3)	16.4	14.5
MELAs (1 + 2 + 3)	95.7	95.9
Outside MELAs	4.3	4.1

(*Source*: adapted from Drewett *et al.*, 1975)

Figure 1.1 shows the distribution of SMLAs.

1. Why does the map only show the SMLAs, and not the MELAs? Remind yourself of the difference between the two, and explain why the inclusion of the outer metropolitan rings makes the map more difficult to understand because it is so general.

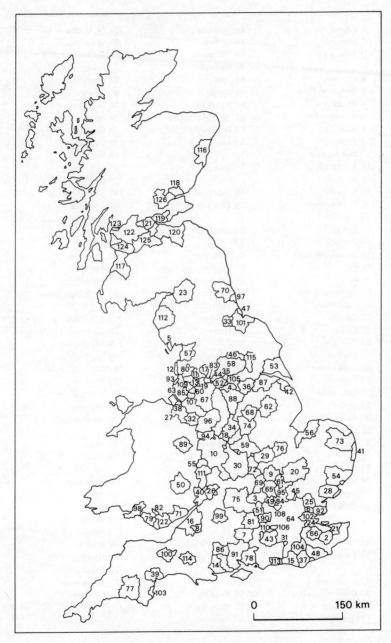

Figure 1.1   Great Britain: standard metropolitan labour areas

1 Aldershot	44 Halifax	84 St Albans
2 Ashford	45 Harlow	85 St Helens
3 Aylesbury	46 Harrogate	86 Salisbury
	47 Hartlepool	87 Scunthorpe
4 Barnsley	48 Hastings	88 Sheffield
5 Barrow-in-Furness	49 Hemel Hempstead	89 Shrewsbury
6 Basildon	50 Hereford	90 Slough
7 Basingstoke	51 High Wycombe	91 Southampton
8 Bath	52 Huddersfield	92 Southend
9 Bedford	53 Hull	93 Southport
10 Birmingham		94 Stafford
11 Blackburn	54 Ipswich	95 Stevenage
12 Blackpool		96 Stoke
13 Bolton	55 Kidderminster	97 Sunderland
14 Bournemouth	56 King's Lynn	98 Swansea
15 Brighton		99 Swindon
16 Bristol	57 Lancaster	
17 Burnley	58 Leeds	100 Taunton
18 Burton on Trent	59 Leicester	101 Teesside
19 Bury	60 Leigh	102 Thurrock
	61 Letchworth	103 Torquay
20 Cambridge	62 Lincoln	104 Tunbridge Wells
21 Canterbury	63 Liverpool	
22 Cardiff	64 London	105 Wakefield
23 Carlisle	65 Luton	106 Walton & Weybridge
24 Chatham		107 Warrington
25 Chelmsford	66 Maidstone	108 Watford
26 Cheltenham	67 Manchester	109 Wigan
27 Chester	68 Mansfield	110 Woking
28 Colchester	69 Milton Keynes	111 Worcester
29 Corby		112 Workington
30 Coventry	70 Newcastle	113 Worthing
31 Crawley	71 Newport	
32 Crewe	72 Northampton	114 Yeovil
	73 Norwich	115 York
33 Darlington	74 Nottingham	
34 Derby		116 Aberdeen
35 Dewsbury	75 Oxford	117 Ayr
36 Doncaster		118 Dundee
	76 Peterborough	119 Dunfermline
37 Eastbourne	77 Plymouth	120 Edinburgh
38 Ellesmere Port	78 Portsmouth	121 Falkirk
39 Exeter	79 Port Talbot	122 Glasgow
	80 Preston	123 Greenock
40 Gloucester		124 Kilmarnock
41 Great Yarmouth	81 Reading	125 Motherwell
42 Grimsby	82 Rhondda	126 Perth
43 Guildford	83 Rochdale	

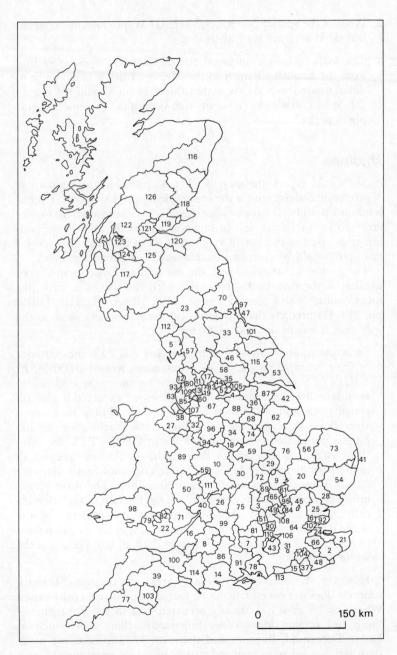

*Figure 1.2   Great Britain: metropolitan economic labour areas (*Source: *Hall and Hay, 1980)*

2. What is the spatial pattern of SMLAs? Where are they concentrated? Where are they absent?

3. The map reveals a continual stretch of urban area, extending from the English Channel to the Mersey. Does it make sense to differentiate the SMLAs within this area, or should we simply call it one CONURBATION, or MEGALOPOLIS, as some geographers prefer?

Discussion

As we would expect, the map of SMLAs picks out the main areas of economic activity within the county, leaving only the rural, highland and peripheral areas as 'unclassified'. (Remember that quite large areas of territory will be included within the outer metropolitan rings; part of the Isle of Wight and all of the Peak District, for example, would be classified in this way, as figure 1.2 shows.)

The problem that arises with the use of the MELA map is very similar to the drawbacks that arise with the use of a term like megalopolis, which means 'great city'. Peter Haggett (1979, pp. 340–41) predicts that the term will become widely used, in the way that it has in the United States:

> Some geographers argue that by the year AD 2000 the existence of three principal megalopolises – sometimes termed *BOSWASH*, *CHIPITTS* and *SANSAN* – will have become more evident. By that date three gargantuan megalopolises are expected to contain roughly one half of the total US population. If they are correct, then Boswash, extending from Boston to Washington, should have a population of around 80 million; CHIPITTS, the lakeshore strip from Chicago to Pittsburgh, should have around 40 million people; and SANSAN, stretching from Santa Barbara to San Diego, should have around 20 million. The three megalopolises would probably contain a large fraction of the scientifically most advanced and most prosperous segments of the world's population: even today, the smallest of the megalopolises (SANSAN) has a larger total income than all but a dozen of the world's nations.

However, the simple fact that large areas will disappear beneath concrete does not necessarily mean that a single urban entity exists. Where coalescence has already occurred – as in the Ruhrgebiet – there still remain identifiable, functional urban areas, such as Essen, Dortmund, Bochum and the rest. By functional, we mean that each town has its own industries, its own commuters, its own shops – in short its own daily urban system. That is why we have concentrated on SMLAs and MELAs here, in order to go beyond the superficial appearance of megalopolis towards the identification of the real patterns of urbanisation which in the British case consist of the 126 tightly meshed but distinct SMLAs.

1.3 The evolution of the British urban system

The urban system is not a static phenomenon. As we showed in our discussion of migration in Book 2, the nineteenth century saw enormous shifts of population on both local and national scales. During the twentieth century, such massive spatial changes have not been repeated, although it is clear that in the last 20 years, the pace of change has again quickened.

An example of the nature of change is revealed in table 1.2 in which the *regional* distributions of population and employment are displayed.

The table shows that during the 1950s all regions experienced growth in both population and employment in their SMLAs. This growth was by no means evenly spread, however. Growth was more marked in the south, East Anglia and the Midlands and was retarded in the north and Scotland. In the 1960s this differential growth had become more pronounced. Although all regions were still growing in terms of urban population, the gap between the relative growth rates of the northwest and East Anglia, for example,

Table 1.2 Population and employment change within SMLAs aggregated to regional totals

Region	Population change (%)		Employment change (%)	
	1951–61	1961–71	1951–61	1961–71
Southeast	7.3	4.4	9.8	2.9
East Anglia	8.7	11.8	10.4	14.5
Yorks–Humberside	3.4	3.6	4.8	−2.0
East Midlands	8.7	9.6	8.6	3.9
West Midlands	7.9	6.6	8.9	1.7
Northwest	1.9	1.9	0.7	−3.6
Northern	5.8	1.7	4.9	2.4
Southwest	8.2	9.5	9.3	8.4
Wales	5.3	4.8	7.7	4.7
Scotland	2.5	0.4	1.6	−2.7
Great Britain total	5.7	4.4	6.7	1.4

Source: Drewett *et al.*, 1975

Table 1.3   Extremes in the ranking of employment change for SMLAs in Great Britain

Table 1.3(a)   1951-61

Top five	Absolute figures	Top five	Per cent
London	263,000	Crawley	658.1
Birmingham	104,200	Harlow	517.4
Coventry	49,500	Basildon	198.7
Luton	27,100	Stevenage	129.2
Bristol	26,400	Hemel Hempstead	72.2

Bottom five	Absolute figures	Bottom five	Per cent
Rhondda	-4,400	Burton	-4.4
Rochdale	-4,700	Rochdale	-7.1
Manchester	-5,000	Leigh	-8.6
Glasgow	-5,600	Warrington	-10.5
Warrington	-10,000	Rhondda	-13.0

Table 1.3(b)   1961-71

Top five	Absolute figures	Top five	Per cent
Portsmouth	32,100	Basildon	100.9
Southampton	32,000	Harlow	86.6
Bristol	25,500	Ellesmere Port	72.2
Basildon	25,400	Basingstoke	72.2
Oxford	25,100	Crawley	60.3

Bottom five	Absolute figures	Bottom five	Per cent
Leeds	-24,000	Manchester	-8.0
Liverpool	-34,100	Halifax	-9.2
Glasgow	-59,700	Burnley	-9.5
Manchester	-84,200	Kilmarnock	-13.7
London	-243,500	Rhondda	-21.0

Source: Drewett *et al.*, 1976

has widened. Furthermore, in the case of employment, Scotland, the northwest and Yorkshire–Humberside's SMLAs actually suffered employment decline. East Anglia was alone in containing SMLAs that experienced a more rapid growth in employment than in population in percentage terms (see also table 1.5).

Figure 1.3 very clearly displays this disparate pattern of growth. The SMLAs receiving below average population growth are clustered in central Scotland and northern England, while the high growth regions are in the Midlands, East Anglia and the south. It will be seen from the map, however, that there are important exceptions to this general statement, most notably London, which experienced below average population growth in the period 1951–71, putting it into the same class as the predominantly northern SMLAs with their consistently low growth rates.

The real nature of the change that London underwent during this 20-year period is far more dramatic than the map alone would suggest. The tables above show the top five and the bottom five SMLAs in the ranking of employment change for the periods 1951–61 and 1961–71. (Table 1.3(a) and 1.3(b); see also table 1.6.)

1. Study tables 1.3(a) and 1.3(b), and with the help of figure 1.1 make sure you can locate each SMLA. An outline map may be useful on which to record this information.

2. In all there are 126 SMLAs recognised in Britain. By how many places has London slipped in the rank order of employment change between tables 1.3(a) and 1.3(b)?

3. With reference to table 1.3(a), explain the differences between the top five SMLAs as measured by absolute changes and relative (percentage) changes.

4. Attempt to explain the decline in employment recorded for the bottom five SMLAs in absolute and percentage figures and for both time periods (1951–61, 1961–71).

Discussion

Within the 20-year period covered by table 1.3, London slipped from first to last in the rank order of change, the full 126 places. Although London gained over 260,000 jobs during the 1950s, in the 1960s it became a rapidly declining urban area so far as employment was concerned. In this sense, London had become similar to other large SMLAs, such as Manchester and Glasgow in the north of Britain, in experiencing major job losses: the only difference was that London's job losses were far greater in absolute terms. In percentage terms, London's decline does not show up quite so dramatically. In both time periods the bottom places of the rank order were dominated by smaller SMLAs in which significant job

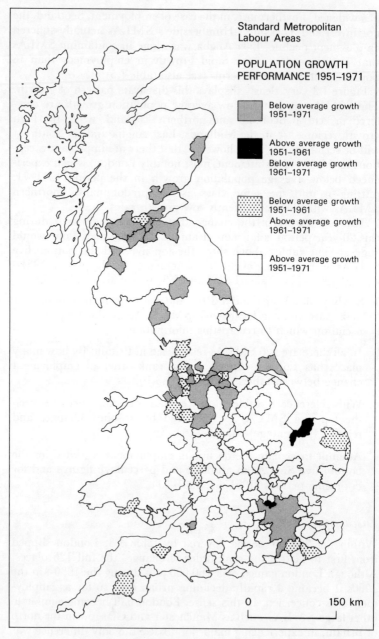

Figure 1.3   SMLA population change, 1951–1971 (Source: Drewett, Goddard and Spence, 1975)

losses show up as large percentage changes. Usually, such SMLAs had clear reasons for their industrial decline. Rhondda, at the bottom of the rank order for the whole 20-year period, was suffering the catastrophic decline of coalmining, whereas Halifax and Rochdale were witnessing the decline of the textile industry. In general terms, then, urban areas experiencing major job losses were the coalfield-based, traditional industrial centres dominated by old, heavy and declining industries in the north of England, Scotland and South Wales.

Although we have commented on the dramatic changes in fortune for the London SMLA between 1951 and 1971, we have barely offered any explanation for it. Also, to be realistic, we cannot really account for job losses in the other large metropolitan SMLAs (like Manchester or Liverpool) solely in terms of 'the decline of heavy industries'. For a full explanation, we must also take into account the factor of population and employment *decentralisation*. This has manifested itself in two ways:

1. In all the major SMLAs, there has been a movement of both jobs and people out of the cores and inner rings (the SMLAs) to the outer rings. In the case of Manchester, this means the expansion of employment in places like Marple. (This area is shown in figure 2.3 in Book 1, *The Region.*)

2. This decentralisation has also been assisted by the planned growth of new settlements, designed specifically to attract and house population. In London for example, growth has gone beyond the outer metropolitan ring to places like Harlow New Town. As table 1.3 show, between 1951–61 the latter grew by 517.4 per cent, and between 1961–71 a still respectable 86.6 per cent. As the table also shows, between 1951–61 all the top five SMLAs in terms of expansion were southeast new towns. Of course, these planned settlements are not only concentrated south of the Wash. We can in fact attribute *some* of the loss of both population and jobs in Glasgow, Manchester and Liverpool to planned settlements, such as East Kilbride, Skelmersdale and Runcorn.

The new towns (and their younger brothers and sisters, the expanded towns and the overspill 'townships') are so different from the other 'natural' components of the British urban system that we need to examine them in detail.

1.4 The planned settlements, 1945–1978

The new towns were part of the major social revolution that began in the postwar era, when a decayed Britain began to rebuild itself.

The chronology is described by Peter Hall (1975, p. 112):

> The first new town, Stevenage, was designated on 11 November 1946 . . . between 1946 and 1950, no less than 14 new towns were designated in England and Wales, 8 of them around London, to serve London overspill, as proposed in the Abercrombie Plan of 1944 (though not always in the locations proposed in the plan, some of which were found to be unsuitable), 2 in North-East England to serve the development area, 1 in South Wales to serve a similar purpose (though it was actually just outside the development area), 2 in Central Scotland for the same reason (1 of which also received overspill from Glasgow), and lastly 1 attached to a prewar steelworks. Then for a decade progress almost ceased: from 1950 to 1961, only 1 new town – Cumbernauld in Scotland – was designated, and in 1957 there was an announcement that no more new towns would be started. But in 1961 there was an abrupt reversal of policy . . . and between then and 1970 no less than 14 further new towns were designated in Great Britain. In 1971, [after] a quarter of a century, Britain's new towns contained close to one million people, with over 180,000 new houses built since designation.

The distribution of new towns is shown in figure 1.4, including their projected size and date of establishment. Since 1970, little has happened to produce further growth. Late arrivals, such as Stonehouse, have been killed off, and in 1978, the annual subsidy of £350 million was removed and redirected towards the inner cities.

1. Examine the distribution of the new towns in figure 1.4. Using Peter Hall's text, divide the towns into two groups, each with a specific and very different function.

2. To what extent do these two groups have (a) specific geographical locations, (b) different dates of designation?

3. Why was there only one new town scheduled between 1950 and 1961, and why did the programme receive new impetus post-1961?

4. Why are there no more new towns in prospect in the foreseeable future?

Discussion

To understand fully the history of the new towns, we have to bear in mind two distinct and separate factors. The first was the condition of British cities post-1945. In many urban areas, the devastation of the war had necessitated drastic surgery of the Victorian urban fabric – a ruthless clearance of the old, poor-

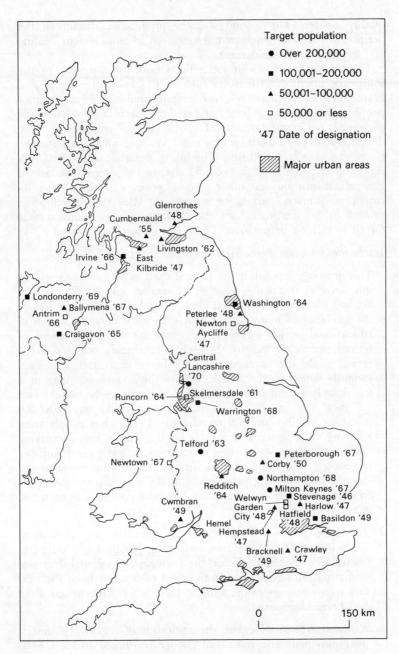

Figure 1.4   New towns and other planned settlements (Source: *Hall, 1975*)

quality houses. The second was the progressive decline of the peripheral regions, which manifested itself in employment decline and increasing unemployment.

The first wave of new towns reflects both these trends. In the southeast, planned settlements such as Bracknell, Stevenage and Hatfield were designed to receive overspill population from London – people whose homes were bulldozed as part of the wholesale clearance of inner London. Elsewhere, the settlements were designed to act as a focus for new employment growth – in Peterlee, Cwmbran and East Kilbride. The lull in designation in the 1950s represented two things; a political change in government, and a general assumption that other regional policies (such as the relocation of industry) would be successful. The latter assumption proved to be incorrect, and the Conservative government was forced to rethink its position. Three factors were recognised.

1. *Household Change* Peter Hall describes it thus (1975, p. 158):

> This growing population . . . proved itself to be splitting itself up into an ever-increasing number of smaller and smaller households – the product of social changes such as earlier marriages, the tendency of many young people to leave home in search of educational or job opportunities, and the increasing trend of retired people to live by themselves in seaside colonies. As a result, while the average size of a home in Britain remained roughly constant, the average size of the household living in it fell sharply: in England and Wales, the average household had 3.7 members in 1931, 3.2 members in 1951, but only 3.0 members in 1961 and 2.9 members in 1971. Thus people were enjoying more space within their homes, but an ever-increasing number of homes was needed to accommodate any given number of people. Reinforcing the rise in population, this trend meant that the total housing programme, and the consequent demands on space, were much greater than had been comfortably assumed in the late 1940s.

2. *Population movement* Throughout the conurbations, movement was widespread; as clearance continued, population left the city centres. Furthermore, within the southeast, a regional drift was occurring, alongside the immigration of families from the new and old commonwealth. Simply, there were more people than had been anticipated.

3. *Regional disparities* Despite the optimism of regional planners, unemployment and industrial change continued to hit Ulster, the north, Scotland and Wales particularly hard. The 'stick and carrot' policies of controlling industrial expansion in the

Midlands and southeast, and attempting to direct development to the periphery, were not a success.

The net effect of these changes was a second round of PLANNED SETTLEMENTS, new and expanded towns in the southeast (Milton Keynes, Northampton and Peterborough) and new towns in the development areas (Warrington, Washington, Londonderry).

Since 1971, the new town story has entered a new phase. For some of the planned settlements, growth continues, and as table 1.6 indicates, the top three growth rates 1971–81 were found in new towns. For others, the period saw either the attainment of the target population (for example, Harlow), or the sudden withdrawal of government funds. The growth of unemployment in the conurbations has caused a redirection of priorities, and as a result, money.

Table 1.4   New towns in England and Wales with populations greater than 50,000: change 1971–81

New towns	1981 population	1971	% Change
Northampton	156,848	133,673	17.3
Basildon	152,301	129,422	17.7
Warrington	135,568	127,648	6.2
Peterborough	115,410	88,082	31.0
Milton Keynes	106,974	52,946	102.0
Telford	103,786	79,594	30.4
Hemel Hempstead	79,695	72,431	10.0
Harlow	79,276	78,105	1.5
Stevenage	74,381	67,094	10.9
Crawley	73,081	69,342	6.9
Redditch	66,854	40,996	63.1
Runcorn	64,117	35,999	78.1
Chorley (C. Lancashire)	54,775	44,887	
Washington	53,783	26,545	102.6

1.5   A perspective on the British urban system

In this chapter we have attempted to cover an enormous amount of information – after all, talking about the British urban system is another way of describing virtually the entire British population. As a result we have had to be very general, and we have glossed over some ideas; the *reasons* for decentralisation are a good deal more complicated than we can discuss here and we shall examine them fully in the next book (*The City*). We must also make some additional comments about the process of urban change itself. It does not stop and it is important that we bring this outline up to date.

In table 1.5, we show the gross patterns of change for settlements with more than 50,000 inhabitants. The figures are, therefore, not strictly comparable with those for the SMLAs in table 1.2 (1981 data for SMLAs do not yet exist) but the clear trends taking place between 1951–71 seem to have continued between 1971 and 1981. The regions with the biggest urban population gains – East Anglia and the East Midlands – have maintained their substantial rate of increase, despite the fact that the national population total for 1971–81 has remained virtually static (increasing only by 0.5 per cent). Over the decade, the population in towns declined by 739,000 (1.9 per cent) for the country as a whole; the population of London, for instance, fell to 6.6 million, the first time it has dropped below 7 million inhabitants since 1901, and its continued decline turns the southeast's slight increase into a net urban decline.

In table 1.6, we show the settlements registering the largest proportions of growth and decline over the decade. Once more, London dominates the lists of shrinking settlements, which is still essentially a list of the major conurbations. As we might now expect, the centres of growth are closely tied to new town policy, although as with table 1.3, we must take account of both percentage and absolute figures, as it is easy to find large proportionate changes in small settlements (cf. St Ives).

Table 1.5   Changes in urban population (towns greater than 50,000) 1971–81, by region

East Anglia	4.1%
East Midlands	3.4%
South East (excluding London)	1.1%
South East (including London)	−2.1%
West Midlands	−1.9%
South West	−2.0%
Wales	−4.9%
Yorkshire	−5.4%
Northern	−5.7%
North West	−8.1%

One additional comment is in order. Britain is not typical of the whole world in the ways in which its urbanisation is evolving. In many developing countries, rapid growth in major centres is the

Table 1.6 Urban areas registering major population changes, 1971–81

Top five	Absolute figures	Top five	Per cent
Milton Keynes	54,031	Washington	+102.6%
Runcorn	28,118	Milton Keynes	+102.0%
Peterborough	27,328	Runcorn	+78.1%
Washington	27,238	St Ives	+71.8%
Redditch	25,858	Redditch	+63.1%

Bottom five	Absolute figures	Bottom five	Per cent
Leeds	−47,481	Bangor	−16.4%
Birmingham	−94,281	Liverpool	−16.4%
Manchester	−96,691	Manchester	−17.4%
Liverpool	−99,807	Gateshead	−21.0%
London	−760,095	Salford	−25.2%

norm. Even in the developed world, there are many different
trends. Japan, for example, is still centralising its population.
America is very similar in appearance to the British trend. Main-
land Europe is rather different, and it is possible that very basic
differences between countries affect the trend of urbanisation (Hall
and Hay 1980, p. 231):

> The most likely hypothesis is that the main differences are
> related to stages of industrial urban evolution, and that as this
> proceeds, Europe will more and more follow the American–British
> path. But the patterns may not be exactly parallel, for at least
> two main reasons. First, cultural styles are different: France and
> the Mediterranean countries have a quite different preference for
> high-density, inner-city apartment-house living, compared with
> the Anglo-American suburban tradition. Second, and even more
> important, much of Europe's urban population is still only one
> or two generations removed from the land, in a way that is
> simply not true for either Great Britain or the United States.
> Many urban families have ancestral farm houses in the country-
> side to which they can return – whether for summer, for week-
> ends, or for retirement, or for an escape from urban pressures to
> a simpler life-style. The return migration to Italy's Mezzogiorno,
> which is such a striking new feature of the 1970–75 analysis,
> offers a foretaste of what could happen if a prolonged recession
> were to limit job opportunities in the larger industrial cities of
> Europe.

Key issues

THE URBAN SYSTEM The towns and cities of Britain are often portrayed on maps as dots, this giving the impression of each urban settlement being a separate entity in the landscape. In reality each urban settlement has a hinterland or field of influence around it containing shoppers and commuters – an area that is 'served' by the town or city. Furthermore, these fields of influence, or *metropolitan rings* as we have called them, are themselves not separate entities and interlock a great deal. Thus, we have a vast, interlocking urban web that accounts for over 95 per cent of the British population – the British urban system.

CONURBATIONS The phenomenal population movements from countryside to town during the nineteenth century, causing rapid expansion of settlements in some favoured areas (such as in the London Basin and on the northern coalfields), resulted in the coalescence of previously separate towns into single continuous urban areas or conurbations. The conurbations in Britain are Strathclyde, Tyne and Wear, Merseyside, Greater Manchester, West Yorkshire, South Yorkshire, West Midlands and Greater London.

MEGALOPOLIS This term was coined by the geographer Jean Gottman to describe the vast chain of urban settlement, over 600 km long, he envisaged would evolve along the eastern seaboard of the United States. Despite the slowing of the spread of large cities in Britain it is perhaps not impossible to imagine the British megalopolis, the coalescence of the Merseyside, Manchester, Yorkshire, Midlands and London conurbations into an almost continuous urban agglomeration of 20 million people.

PLANNED SETTLEMENTS The recognition of 'urban problems' such as poor housing and overcrowding led to increasing pressures in the latter half of the nineteenth century to improve the standard of urban living. The most influential thinker in this field was without doubt Ebenezer Howard who wrote the book *Garden Cities of Tomorrow* in 1898. The basis of his idea was that to decentralise industry away from the inner sections of towns would enable people to live in an uncongested, pleasant environment. In effect, he proposed that towns should be *planned* to combine the advantages of urban life (notably accessibility and job opportunities) with the advantages of rural life (notably the environment). Both Letchworth (1903) and Welwyn Garden City (1920) were founded on the principles he had suggested. The garden city idea remained the basic principle on which the new towns of the immediate post-second world war period were based. These 'first wave' new towns were built to fulfil two distinct aims, first, to absorb the overspill population from the old city cores, and second, to help generate new jobs in declining industrial regions. The 'second wave' of new towns, in the 1960s, generally had larger target populations (the planned population of Milton Keynes is 200,000 people, compared with Harlow, whose final population is 80,000) but in essence they were still based upon the garden city principle.

The new towns are by no means the only form of planned settlements in Britain. Indeed, many of the 'second wave' new towns were not 'new' in the sense that they were built 'from scratch' on green fields. Northampton, for example, is really an expanded town; it was already a substantial urban settlement in its own right before planned expansion took place. Equally, many local authorities have created smaller overspill communities within their boundaries; examples here might be Kirby (on Merseyside) and Killingworth (Tyne–Wear).

2
Rank-size regularities

2.1 Introduction and definitions

In Chapter 1, we examined the British urban system in an empirical way, that is, we have simply observed the factual outline of the trends in present-day urbanisation. In this chapter (and the next) we want to examine two additional issues, both of which concentrate upon the similarities that exist between cities. In chapter 3, we will examine the regularities of shopping provision within cities with roughly the same populations. In this chapter, we are going to look at the ways in which different countries appear to have very similar proportions of urban places of a particular size. This has come to be called the RANK-SIZE RULE.

It was noted by geographers over half a century ago that in many countries, a similar progression of city sizes exists. We begin to show this by measuring the population of the largest city, the urban place ranked first in terms of population (London, Paris, New York, Tokyo). From this simple measurement, it is then often possible to predict successfully the size of many other settlements within the country. Thus the second-largest city is often found to have half the largest city's population, the third largest has one-third of the population of the largest, and so on. This is easily expressed in mathematical terms:

$$P_i = \frac{P_1}{r_i} \qquad [1]$$

where P_i is the population of the city in which we are interested, P_1 is the population of the largest city, and r_i is the rank of P_i. This mathematical relationship is more usually presented in the form of a graph, on which the populations and the ranks are both plotted. Normally, a LOGARITHMIC SCALE is used, with the result that a straight line relationship emerges, as in figure 2.1.

When we use real data, as in figure 2.2, which shows a rank size plot for the 126 British SMLAs, we can see that the close mathematical progression discussed above is visible *to a certain degree*. Thus, the second-largest SMLA is slightly smaller than we might have predicted using the formula, and the graph as a whole has several kinks in it. Nonetheless, it seems that an approximation of

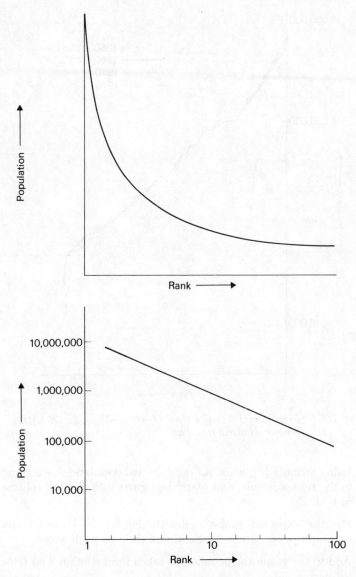

Figure 2.1   The rank-size distribution, using normal and logarithmic scales

a rank size relationship exists (and has existed since 1950) in Britain.

As we have already suggested, the British example is by no means unique. In table 2.1 are data relating to American cities (defined as the population living within the administrative areas).

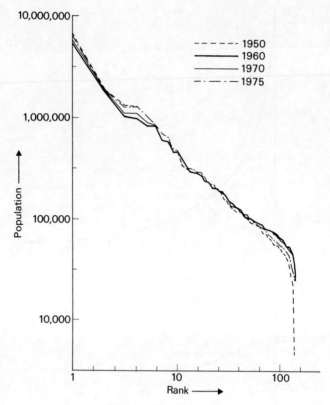

Figure 2.2   Great Britain: rank-size plot 1950–60–70–75 for the 126 SMLAs
(Source: *Hall and Hay, 1980*)

1. Using formula [1], work out the expected populations according to the rank-size rule, and place the figures into the fifth column in table 2.1.

2. Plot the 'expected' rank-size distribution for the United States on graph paper, using a logarithmic scale on each axis.

3. Add to the graph the populations taken from column 3 on table 2.1.

4. Comment on the 'fit' of the data to the expected. Is it closer to the expected than the British data? Can you suggest any reasons for the slight differences?

Table 2.1   The population of the 20 largest American cities, 1975

City	(Rank)	Population (000s)	% change since 1970	Expected population
New York	(1)	7,482	−6.0	
Chicago	(2)	3,099	−8.8	
Los Angeles	(3)	2,727	−2.4	
Philadelphia	(4)	1,816	−7.8	
Houston	(5)	1,397	+13.4	
Detroit	(6)	1,335	−13.2	
Baltimore	(7)	852	−8.6	
Dallas	(8)	822	−0.1	
San Diego	(9)	774	+13.1	
San Antonio	(10)	773	+10.6	
Indianapolis	(11)	725	−2.9	
Washington	(12)	712	−7.5	
Milwaukee	(13)	666	−7.8	
Pheonix	(14=)	665	+15.4	
San Francisco	(14=)	665	−7.3	
Cleveland	(16)	639	−16.7	
Boston	(17)	637	−3.6	
New Orleans	(18)	560	−2.1	
Columbus	(19)	536	−1.3	
St Louis	(20)	525	−16.5	

Source: Geographical Digest 1980

Discussion

The American urban system is highly dynamic. More simply, urbanisation within the United States is still a relatively recent phenomenon, and some of the cities identified in table 2.1 have grown only recently. For example, while nearly half of New York's population growth occurred between 1870 and 1920, other metropolitan areas barely existed during this period. Both Miami and Las Vegas, for instance, have grown as cities entirely since 1920, while Los Angeles has added 85 per cent of its population since that date. As table 2.1 shows, some cities, particularly those in the so-called 'sun belt', are still growing rapidly. The obvious examples are Houston, whose growth is based on oil wealth and the space center, and Pheonix, which is the centre of a large military testing complex. Conversely, many of the long-established cities are losing population, because of crime, high property costs and the rival attractions of growth centres elsewhere in the country. In other words, change is constant, and consequently we should not expect a perfect rank-size distribution; we should, in fact, be surprised that the figures are as good a fit as they are.

2.2 Explaining the rank-size graph

It is one thing to discover a particular relationship; it is, of course, rather more difficult to explain why such a relationship occurs. Many geographers and economists have attempted this task, and in consequence various types of explanation for the rank-size effect have been produced. Many of these are rather complicated, but we can simplify their arguments a good deal.

One of the most interesting studies was carried out just after the Second World War by a professor of German named Zipf. We have already encountered his work before in the field of interaction (Book 2.) Zipf was interested in the fact that some relationships seem to occur in very different fields of knowledge, and in effect he noted that the rank-size distribution is not simply to do with cities. In one of his studies, he counted the numbers of different words in James Joyce's work, *Ulysses*. Some, naturally enough, occurred frequently, while others were used only once or twice. He noted that the distribution could be summarised in the form:

$$fWi = \frac{fW1}{ri} \qquad [2]$$

In other words, the frequency of occurrence (f) of any word W could be found by dividing the most common word by the rank of i; a quick comparison of equations [1] and [2] will show that they are identical in form. For those who doubt that words and cities could be comparable, table 2.2 shows an extract of Zipf's results.

Table 2.2   The frequency of words in James Joyce's Ulysses

Rank	Frequency	Rank	Frequency
10	2,653	5,000	5
20	1,311	10,000	2
30	926	20,000	1
40	717	29,899	1

Source: after Zipf, 1949

Zipf's work suggests therefore that we are dealing with a *statistical* relationship, which means that it is in the nature of different things to conform to the same pattern. The simplest example of a statistical regularity is the NORMAL DISTRIBUTION, which is the usual

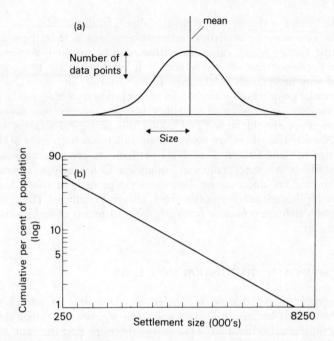

Figure 2.3   *a) The normal distribution. The population is distributed equally
about the mean*
*b) The log-normal distribution. The graph shows the cumulative
proportion of population in settlements larger than the sizes shown
on the bottom axis*

form for many types of data to take. The normal curve is bell-
shaped, as in figure 2.3(a). The average is in the centre of the
distribution, and the extremes extend equally out above and below
this mean value. If we were to survey the male population's height
or foot size, we would find an average height or size (perhaps 5ft
8in. or size 8), with a few individuals possessing large or small feet
(size 2 or size 14) and some being very tall or very small (4ft 8in.
or 6ft 8in.).

If we extend this argument to settlements, it is also likely that
a crude version of the normal distribution would apply; in other
words, there are very few really large cities and relatively few very
small hamlets. The bulk of the population in a society such as
Great Britain lives in settlements between these extremes. The
rank-size distribution, as we have seen, concentrates upon cities
instead of the whole range of settlements, and here a rather
different distribution occurs. Again, there are few large cities, but
rather more small ones. If we measure the cumulative distribution
of population, as in figure 2.3(b), we find that a variant of the

normal curve – the *log-normal* distribution – is applicable.

The reasons why statistical relationships hold is that there are limiting factors which cause the extremes to be unusual. As far as natural phenomena are concerned, it is relatively easy to understand why individuals rarely grow to be very tall, and indeed why very small people rarely survive. In an evolutionary sense, too large = unwieldy, and too small = vulnerable. Settlements, too, evolve, although we should be wary of taking this biological analogy too far. Nonetheless, there are again constraints upon both ends of the population distribution. Very large settlements are also unwieldy and difficult to finance, police and maintain. Conversely, very small settlements are uneconomic, because services such as shops have to be replicated too frequently from village to village. There are thus very definite economic pressures for settlements of certain sizes to emerge.

2.3 The rank-size distribution over time

This type of explanation of settlement sizes has an additional interest for us because it focuses upon *general* processes rather than each individual settlement. This means therefore that the rank-size graph should work for a particular country throughout its urban history.

A great deal of research has been done on the history of British urbanisation by the British geographer Brian Robson. He shows, for example, that during the nineteenth century, a period of intense industrialisation and population migration, the number of towns (places with populations greater than 2,500 people) grew from 256 to 885. Equally, there was a continual trend for settlements to get larger and larger, as industrial activity quickened. In 1801, 62 per cent of the settlements in England and Wales contained between 2,500 and 5,000 people, but by 1901 this had shrunk to fewer than 30 per cent.

As we might expect, these gross figures hide an enormous amount of change as far as individual settlements were concerned. Some, such as mining towns, enjoyed brief spells of growth. Others, such as county (market) towns, were slowly eclipsed by the expansion of the new, industrial settlements. When we examine a rank-population graph for the century as a whole, we find a great deal of 'coming and going'. Figure 2.4 shows that only at the very top of the urban system was there little change; London remained throughout the century the largest city, Manchester and Liverpool simply changed places in the ranking in the middle of the period, and Birmingham remained consistently in fourth place. Below this group, however, enormous flux is evident. For example, Leicester

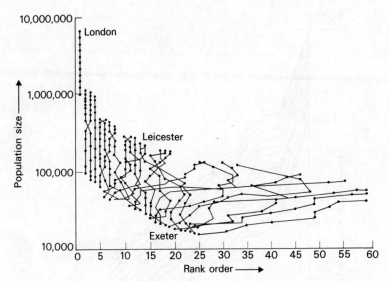

Figure 2.4   *Changes in rank order, 1801–1911. Successive ranks of the 25 largest towns in England and Wales in 1801. Each line represents one town; the lowest dot shows its rank and size in 1801 and successive dots show its rank and size at each decade up to 1911. The towns (ranked in their 1801 order) are as follows: London; Manchester/ Salford; Liverpool; Birmingham; Bristol; Leeds; Portsmouth; Newcastle/Gateshead; Sheffield; Norwich; Bath; Nottingham; Hull; Sunderland; Medway Towns; Stockport; Bolton; Coventry; Exeter; Leicester; York; Plymouth; Oldham; Chester; Oxford.* (Source: *Robson, 1973*)

becomes relatively more important, then less important, and finally finishes ranked twelfth in 1911. Exeter, which began the period ranked alongside Leicester at nineteenth, diminishes dramatically throughout the century, and drops several dozen places.

We emphasised previously that a rank-size graph concentrates upon *overall* relationships, and not individual settlements. It is interesting, therefore, to look at the national graph for this period. As figure 2.5 shows, despite the fact that particular towns and cities were growing or relatively declining, the statistical relationship remained virtually constant throughout the nineteenth century, as displayed by the angle and shape of the curves. Although we may assume that the overall rank-size relationship has remained much the same right up to the present time, it is worth while studying the more recent 'coming and going' in the rank order of British cities. Table 2.3 shows the top 20 cities in Britain according to their populations in 1961, 1971 and 1981, with the exception of London, already discussed above.

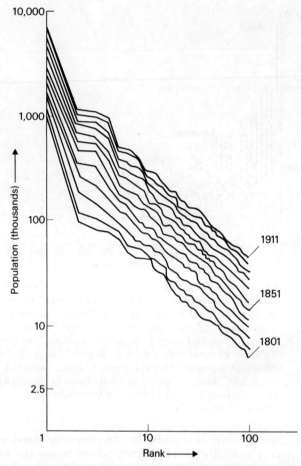

Figure 2.5   The rank-size graph, Britain, 1901–1911. (Source: Robson, 1973)

1. The table shows that the largest cities maintained their positions, with the exception of Sheffield and Manchester, which exchanged positions during the 1970s. Lower down the rank order there has been considerable movement. Draw up three lists to show cities that:
   (a) Moved down the rank order during the 1960s only.
   (b) Moved down the rank order during the 1970s only.
   (c) Moved down the rank order consistently over the 20-year period.

2. Which city dropped the most places during the whole 20-year period?

Table 2.3 Rank order of the top twenty British cities (excluding London)

Rank	1961	1971	1981
1	Birmingham	Birmingham	Birmingham
2	Liverpool	Liverpool	Liverpool
3	Manchester	Manchester	Sheffield
4	Sheffield	Sheffield	Manchester
5	Leeds	Leeds	Leeds
6	Bristol	Bristol	Bristol
7	Coventry	Coventry	Coventry
8	Nottingham	Nottingham	Bradford
9	Hull	Bradford	Leicester
10	Bradford	Cardiff	Cardiff
11	Cardiff	Hull	Nottingham
12	Leicester	Leicester	Hull
13	Stoke	Wolverhampton	Wolverhampton
14	Newcastle	Stoke	Stoke
15	Wolverhampton	Plymouth	Plymouth
16	Plymouth	Newcastle	Derby
17	Sunderland	Derby	Southampton
18	Portsmouth	Sunderland	Sunderland
19	Derby	Southampton	Newcastle
20	Southampton	Portsmouth	Dudley
	(28 Dudley)	(21 Dudley)	(21 Portsmouth)

3. Draw up three lists to show cities that:
   (a) Moved up the rank order during the 1960s.
   (b) Moved up the rank order during the 1970s.
   (c) Moved up the rank order consistently during the whole 20-year period.

4. Which city in the top 20 has risen through the rank order the most during the whole period?

5. For each of the settlements that you have identified in questions 1 to 4, suggest a reason (or reasons) why relative growth or decline has occurred. Is there a single explanation to account for movement up the ranking, and one explanation to account for downward movement, or do different cities invite individual explanations?

Discussion

One point which must be stressed from the outset is that of the 20 largest cities in 1981, 18 had in fact *lost* population over the preceding decade, and 15 had lost population consistently between

1961 and 1981. This means that changes in rank reflect different rates of decline, with only Plymouth and Dudley actually gaining inhabitants. Second, it is useful to differentiate between rank changes which are relatively minor (for example, Stoke, from thirteenth to fourteenth in 1961–81) and those which appear irreversible (for example, Newcastle upon Tyne, from fourteenth in 1961 down to nineteenth 20 years later).

As far as rank decline is concerned, we can identify relatively consistent causes. The cases of Hull and Newcastle upon Tyne, for instance, both reflect the collapse of traditional industries within regions of increasing unemployment. In Newcastle's case, this has resulted in population movement within the Tyneside conurbation, and this type of intra-urban movement is also reflected in other large cities such as Manchester; the demise of Salford (from thirtieth in 1961 to fifty-sixth in 1981) is the most extreme case. Note of course that not all declines are in the 'problem regions'; the contraction of the naval dockyards in Portsmouth reflects a similar process being acted out in an otherwise prosperous area.

The explanations for upward movement are slightly more diverse. From table 2.3, we can pick out settlements like Southampton, which owe a stable population (and a rank increase of three places) to port-related industry and a role as regional growth centre. Plymouth would be a similar example. Dudley, by way of contrast, represents a counterpart to the inner urban decline discussed above; in this outer metropolitan district of the West Midlands, overspill population has produced an absolute increase in numbers. In addition we can also pick out cities like Leicester and Bradford, which have received relatively large numbers of new commonwealth immigrants whose arrival has to some extent offset the decline generally exhibited by settlements of this size.

2.4 Deviations from the rank-size

So far, we have only examined two countries (the United Kingdom and United States), for which the rank-size model is relatively successful. What however of those nations where the balance of population is very different? Table 2.4 indicates that this is by no means unusual.

The table indicates 25 countries where there exists a condition of PRIMACY, that is, an inflated major city, which is more than twice the size of the next-largest settlement (as predicted by the rank-size rule). As an additional measure, the concentration of population in the four largest settlements is also shown, and for comparison, the equivalent figures for the United States and the United Kingdom are included.

Table 2.4   Examples of primate urban patterns: 1955

Country	Ratio of largest to second largest city	Percentage of nation's population living in 4 biggest settlements
Uruguay	10.0	86.7
Hungary	13.2	84.7
Guatemala	12.7	83.9
Paraguay	9.0	83.3
Phillippines	9.8	82.0
Peru	7.3	81.7
Argentina	9.1	79.4
Ceylon	4.6	78.0
Haiti	5.6	77.8
Cuba	7.3	77.3
Austria	7.3	76.8
Denmark	7.7	76.2
Ireland	4.7	75.8
Tunisia	5.9	75.6
Greece	4.9	75.2
France	7.5	74.7
Mexico	7.4	74.3
Thailand	3.5	74.1
Rumania	8.0	73.8
Chile	4.8	71.4
Lebanon	5.5	70.6
United Kingdom	2.7	18.0
United States	2.4	7.0

Source: extracted from Richardson, 1973

1. Which do you regard as the best measure of primacy, the ratio of the two largest settlements' populations, or the percentage living in the four largest settlements? (You may decide that both variables are useful.)

2. Examine the countries listed in table 2.4. What do they have in common? Some of the factors you should consider would include:
   (a) Geographical location.
   (b) Political history.
   (c) Economic development.
   (d) Size; (you may interpret this variable in several ways).
   (e) Political organisation (for example, federal system or centralised system).

3. What can you suggest as possible explanations for the absence of rank-size distributions?

Discussion

There are obvious similarities between the countries listed above. The majority is made up of less industrialised countries (although France should really be considered as an anomaly in this context, both in terms of size and level of development). They are all relatively small, and several have had a colonial past (this is particularly true of the seven Latin American countries). This has caused some writers to suggest that primacy is simply a first stage in the road to full industrialisation and development, although this is questionable on several levels, not least because it assumes that all nations evolve in the same way. Paris, for example, owes its primacy to the strong centralising tendencies of Napoleon's bureaucratic organisation which gave it an unusually important role in France's affairs; however, it would clearly be dangerous to infer anything in the way of a general law from that.

The problems of primacy, and particularly the evolutionary explanation, are summarised by economist Harry Richardson (1973, p. 168):

> The Latin American experience provides an interesting comment on [the] developmental model of city size distributions ... a study of eight countries showed that the reverse situation held – a shift over time from a rank-size distribution to primacy. However, the earlier rank-size distributions could not be interpreted as evidence of an integrated hierarchy but rather suggested a structure of colonial cities in terrain where high communication costs prevented centralisation. The shift towards primacy coincided (apart from the anomalous case of Mexico) with a marked expansion in exports per capita.

This evidence can however be contrasted with the fruits of other studies, as Richardson goes on to argue, with respect to another piece of research (1973, p. 169):

> A more systematic analysis of primate distributions suggested that it is impossible to service a large, spatially-extensive country from one city; that high incomes mean more urban services which cannot be supplied in a rich country from a single city; that in a foreign-oriented export economy the profits from commercial development will be heavily concentrated in the capital or leading trading metropolis; that ex-colonial status may affect primacy, though in either direction, depending on how the colony was administered and developed; that industrialisation

promotes dispersal via the needs of industries and population to be located near raw materials and power sources; and that rapid population growth will be associated with primacy because of both high rates of natural increase in the metropolis and of rural urban migration.

We may be forgiven for being a little confused at this point concerning primacy versus the rank-size distribution, and it is time to restate the usefulness of the latter approach. As far as a population distribution throughout a country's towns and cities is concerned, it is simplest to assume that a rank-size effect will be found – except where there are good reasons for it not to. Remember, we have suggested that it is a statistical regularity, not a process. Consequently, it will be found only when there are no other, specific processes, like colonial rule or poor communications, to upset the regularity. In some countries, a rank-size regularity may degenerate into primacy, in others the opposite may occur, as the process causing one settlement to grow ceases to operate. As a test of our statement, you should now re-examine the data in table 2.4.

1. The figures used above are for 1955. Using sources such as the *Geographical Digest* and the *Penguin World Atlas* (Hall 1979), recompute the ratios and percentages for each country for a more recent date.

2. Divide the countries into two groups, those becoming *more* primate, and those *less* so.

3. Examine the changes in the gross national product (GNP) of these groups of countries. Is there any evidence that economic progress consistently produces changes in the population distribution? Is there any evidence that other factors are also important? Does the physical geography, for example, appear to play a consistent role?

Key issues

THE RANK-SIZE RULE When the settlements of a country are examined (on a national scale rather than on a regional scale) a statistical regularity is often observed, best described by the expressions found in section 2.1. In other words, the second-largest city in the country is approximately half the size of the largest, the third largest is roughly one-third the size of the largest, the fourth a quarter the size, and so on. It is important to remember that this is an observation and not a theory, in the sense that it helps us to explain or understand cities. Many phenomena display statistical regularity in this way; it is simply a 'way of the world'. However, when the settlements of a country do not conform to the rule, we are justified in seeking special explanations as to why – and it is for this reason that realising that settlements should normally conform to the rank-size rule is important.

LOGARITHMIC SCALE Using a logarithmic scale on the axes of a graph enables data with large spread to be plotted. (see figure 2.1.)

NORMAL DISTRIBUTION For a full explanation refer to a text on the use of statistics such as *Science in Geography* Nos 3 and 4 (Davies, 1974, McCullagh, 1974). In brief we can say here that the frequency distribution of 'normal' data forms a symmetrical bell-shaped curve as in figure 2.3. Much of statistics – often described as the 'mathematics of probability' – is based upon the assumption that data are 'normally distributed'. Thus, if we assume that the heights of people in your year group at school form a normal distribution and a member of the year group is selected at random, the most *probable* height for this individual would be on or near the mean, and it is most unlikely that he or she would be exceptionally large, or small.

HIERARCHY The form of hierarchy can best be visualised with the help of a diagram and, as the following diagram shows, hierarchy is an organisational structure:

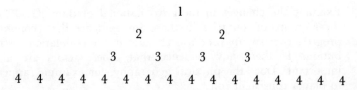

1. Headmaster/mistress/Principal
2. deputy headmaster/mistress
3. Heads of house (year heads)
4. Group tutors (form tutors)

In this case, the organisational structure of a school is illustrated and we talk about certain groups of teachers at a certain level of the hierarchy. Settlements are similarly organised, with different size groupings being at different levels in the hierarchical structure. Christaller, discussed in Chapters 3 and 4, adds a spatial dimension to this organisational structure.

PRIMACY We have emphasised that it is normal to expect the settlements of a country to conform to the rank-size rule. There are many exceptions, however, and probably the most striking type of exception is when the largest settlement is far larger than it 'should' be. When this occurs, as it does in France and seems to in many Third World countries, it is referred to as a state of primacy. As this condition is *not* what we would expect (because it does not conform to the 'normal' statistical regularity) we are justified in seeking special explanations for it.

3
Central place theory

3.1 Central place theory (CPT) – a geographical theory

If, as we have seen, the rank-size distribution is a statistical regularity, it is also worth considering whether there exist any specifically *geographical* approaches to settlement sizes. Of course, there are several, and the most famous of these is CENTRAL PLACE THEORY, originally developed by another German theoretician, Walter Christaller. His work was originally undertaken in south Germany in the 1930s, and was only translated into English in 1966. It is now however universally regarded as one of the subject's most successful achievements. One American geographer, Bill Bunge (1962, p. 133), has written, 'If it were not for the existence of central place theory, it would not be possible to be so emphatic about the existence of a theoretical geography ... central place theory is geography's finest intellectual product'.

CPT takes us along a very different path from the rank-size notion, for several reasons:

1. On account of the type of explanations involved.
2. Because it suggests a very different structure of urban places, that is, a HIERARCHY.
3. Because of the type of theory it represents (note Bunge's comments above).
4. On account of its spatial component.

Let us begin to examine the basic constructs of CPT, in the above order.

Central place theory does not deal solely with urban populations; instead it focuses upon both population *and* retail provision, the number and types of shops. In this sense, CPT takes a very specific view of *why* settlements come into being at all, with the marketing function being heavily stressed.

As soon as urbanisation is assumed to result from a particular process, it is unlikely that a simple rank-size distribution is to be expected. A simple analogy may underline this. Consider the distribution of educational institutions in one town. What is the form of the distribution? Is it a smooth curve, with one very large institution (say a university), two colleges (of half the size), three comprehensives and so on? Obviously not. The distribution is far more structured, as different institutions work better with different numbers of students. Primary schools are small and frequent, comprehensives are larger and less frequent, whilst universities are very large and thus infrequent. Clearly this is not a smooth distribution, but a hierarchy.

When we return to retail provision, we find similar constraints which produce equally predictable results. These constraints are to do with the profitability of retail outlets on the one hand, and individual mobility on the other. In Book 2, *Interaction*, we discussed these issues, showing that each individual possesses an action space, beyond which (s)he rarely travels, and that each commercial activity (such as a cinema) has a demand zone, or sphere of influence, beyond which it draws little or no trade. Let us now put these two concepts together.

Assume for the moment a sparsely inhabited area, as in figure 3.1(a). People live here in scattered homes; they require goods and services. Clearly, some shops are required. One possibility would be to locate them all in one place, creating a very large collection of retailers (figure 3.1(b)). However, this might be inaccessible to some residents. An alternative would be to take mobility into account, and to locate shops near to every home. In this case however, there would not be enough business to allow the individual shops to operate (figure 3.1(c)). In consequence, a compromise is normal. Numbers of shops grow up, which are far enough apart to be profitable, but not too far apart for consumers to have mobility problems. Respectively, we term these constraints the THRESHOLD and the RANGE OF A GOOD (for definitions, see key issues, and for examples of ranges, see table 4.2.) For any particular type of product, both the range and the threshold will be predictable; it is unusual, for example, to find a Boots chemists shop without a local supporting population in excess of 10,000 people.

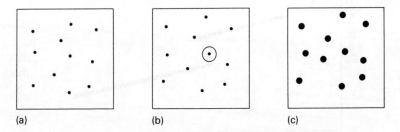

(a) (b) (c)

Figure 3.1 a) *Sparsely inhabited area*
b) *One major retailing settlement*
c) *Numerous small retail outlets*

Conversely, the evidence is that shoppers in this country are rarely prepared to travel more than a mile to buy everyday goods like bread and vegetables.

These two opposing forces produce in consequence a sorting of settlement sizes, in the same way that our school analogy was seen

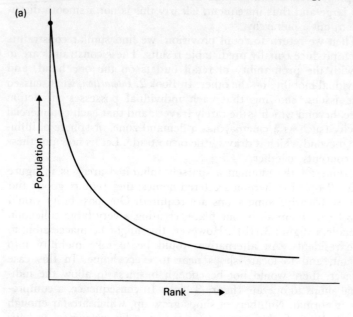

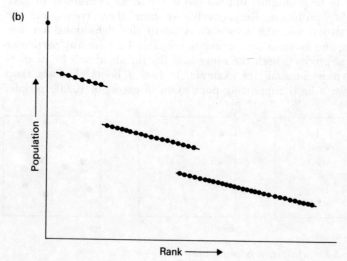

Figure 3.2   The rank-size curve (a) contrasted with an urban hierarchy (b)

to operate. In the first instance, we might find that all food shops require a threshold level of 500 customers. Consequently, for approximately every 500 people in an area, there will be one bread shop, one grocer, and so on. To take this to its logical conclusion, for approximately every 500 people in an area, there will be one settlement supplying a range of these low-level food supplies. We can take this much further. Furniture and clothing stores may require a threshold of 10,000 people. For every 10,000 or so people, a settlement containing these types of goods will exist, while even more expensive goods (luxury items like some cars and jewellery) may require a threshold of 100,000 people. This will clearly involve a greater amount of travelling for consumers, but such goods have a far greater range due to their sheer cost and infrequency of the purchase.

If we return to our hypothetical region in figure 3.1, we can expect a very ordered set of settlements. If there are 100,000 residents in the area, we would expect the following settlement structure:

1 settlement supplying 'high-order' goods;
10 settlements supplying 'medium-order' goods;
200 settlements supplying 'low-order' goods.

(As we shall see below, *all* 211 settlements supply low-order goods, in addition to any medium- or higher- order goods.) This means that groups of roughly similar-sized settlements are expected, in the manner of figure 3.2(b). Here we can see a definite hierarchy, within this example three 'steps', which is of course a very different situation from that outlined in the now-familiar rank-size case (figure 3.2(a))

3.2 CPT and the rank-size

It is in the nature of many subjects to present alternative explanations for the same observable phenomena, although as disciplines evolve, these are usually discarded, one by one. Occasionally, however, a situation arises in which different explanations are used side by side. In physics, for example, debate on the nature of light can be traced back to Pythagoras and Aristotle, with the former arguing that light travels in short bursts, or particles, whilst the latter argued that its motion was more akin to waves. These two views have existed concurrently throughout two millenia, and in fact neither can be disproved due to the problem of experimental observation; the notion of light travelling as both particles *and* waves is now embodied in quantum theory.

CPT and the rank-size rule can hardly be compared with the physics of light in terms of the intellectual debate that they have produced, but it is important that we understand quite why we can use two approaches which appear to contradict each other. Basically, there are two issues to consider.

1. SPATIAL SCALE A fundamental point rarely noted with respect to the two approaches is that they deal with very different geographical scales. The rank-size data examined in Chapter 2 were concerned with individual nations, and our discussion has concentrated upon explanations at that scale. (Some would argue that this is incorrect, and that, for example, Russian cities belong to a different urban system than do other settlements in the far east of the Soviet Union. We should in fact be alive to the possibility that what is a nation today was not a nation when the urban system evolved.)

   In contrast, the basis of central place theory is an understanding of marketing behaviour, which in the main is carried

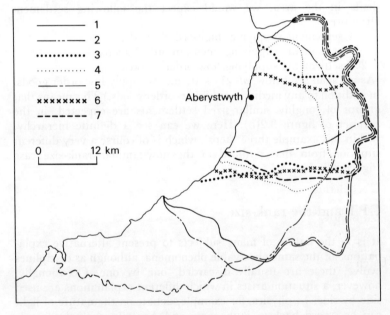

Figure 3.3   Various methods of delimiting trade areas around an urban area (after
             Carter, 1980). The measures are:
             1 An insurance company's office area
             2 A baker's delivery area
             3 An agricultural cooperative delivery area
             4 A bank area
             5 A school catchment area
             6 A postal district
             7 A vetinary surgeon's area

on within relatively small geographical areas. We can for example, pick out a distinct trading area around any settlement, beyond which few retailing trips will normally be made. Figure 3.3 indicates such a catchment for Aberystwyth.

The small scale of most CPTsystems thus means that they are normally considered at the *regional*, rather than the national scale. Even London, which of course functions as an international centre for some activities (such as insurance), can hardly be said to constitute a national shopping centre for any but the wealthiest customers. Consequently, when we look back to figure 3.2, we can see that one way to reconcile the different forms of the population/rank graph is to assume that the smooth curve is a *national* graph, and the stepped hierarchy a *regional* graph.

(*a*) Using data from the *Geographical Digest*, examine the urban system for the German Federal Republic (BRD) and the German Democratic Republic (DDR). Do either of them conform to a recognisable urban pattern; (primacy, rank-size)? Repeat your calculations, using the fifteen largest settlements from *both* countries (table 3.1). Does this give a better fit? Why is it legitimate to manipulate the data in this cavalier way?

Table 3.1   Fifteen largest urban settlements in BRD and DDR; 1976

BRD (*West Germany*) (*'000s*)		DDR (*East Germany*) (*'000s*)
(West Berlin 1,951)	Berlin 3,652	(East Berlin 1,701)
Hamburg	1,699	
München	1,315	
Köln	981	
Essen	670	
Frankfurt	626	
Dortmund	624	
Düsseldorf	615	
Stuttgart	590	
Duisburg	582	Leipzig 566
Bremen	568	
Hannover	547	
Nürnberg	499	
Bochum	413	

Source: Geographical Digest, 1980

(b) Make a list of countries which have undergone major
boundary changes and which have made their urban
systems either smaller (such as in the case of Germany) or
larger (such as the Soviet Union). How quickly do you think
an urban system changes to compensate for such amputa-
tions or additions? (Examples you might consider are
Austria and Norway–Sweden.)

(c) What is the relationship between regional hierarchies and
the national rank-size distribution? What happens when
many separate stepped hierarchies from different regions are
superimposed? If they are all identical in terms of population
size, one composite hierarchy will remain. However, if all the
different hierarchies vary a little in terms of population, then
the clear pattern seen in figure 2.4 is likely to disappear.
Using data from table 3.2, you can see that urban places
with very similar sets of functions (that is, on the same level
within the hierarchy) can vary quite dramatically in size
(due to many local factors, such as transportation functions,
military establishments, entertainment attractions and so
on).

Table 3.2   *Variations in population between same-order settlements,
Washington, USA*

Location in hierarchy	Settlement	Population
First order settlements	Marysville	2,460
(department stores;	Snohomish	3,494
clinics; accountants)	Arlington	1,915
	Monroe	1,684
Second order settlements	Darrington	974
(dentists; banks; hotels)	Granite Falls	600
	Lynnwood	500
	East Stanwood	390
Third order settlements	Lowell	1,600
(restaurants; garages;	Beverly Park	725
churches)	Florence	300
	Silverton	15

Source: adapted from Berry and Garrison, 1958

Once more, we arrive at a statistical relationship, the product
of slight variations within the many regional hierarchies together
producing a blurred, even smooth curve.

2. *Types of theories* A second major difference between the CPT and rank-size approaches is the theoretical assumptions upon which they are based. The rank-size distribution is *inductive*, an empirical regularity, that is, it has been observed in different countries, and various conjectures have been made as to how it comes about. Because it is an observed phenomenon, there can be no explanation which can be 'proved' to be correct, and indeed Richardson discusses 13 equally plausible ways of accounting for rank-size regularities.

In the terms of the philosophy of science, this makes such an approach a *descriptive theory*. This is very different from central place theory, which was developed entirely *deductively*, step by step, one logical proposition following another. In scientific terminology, this makes it a *positive theory*. (There is a third type of theory, known as *normative*, which we will examine in Chapter 4.) Peter Hall outlines the differences between these types of theory as follows (1974, pp. 48–49):

> The simplest possible division, is between normative theory and descriptive theory. One may ask how people and groups should act in order to get the best results ['normative theory']; or one may ask how people actually go about getting the results they do, whether admirable or not ['descriptive theory']. But then, borrowing also from the language of economics, one may speak of a third type; positive theory. Like normative theory, this is deductive in that it starts from certain rules or premises. But like descriptive theory, it seeks to explain what will happen under certain conditions, not what should happen. Nevertheless, because it has an inherent logical structure, it provides an implicit guide to policy-makers in that it seeks to show them the consequences of alternative policy actions.
>
> This three-fold classification is I believe the most useful one. It is not always easy to decide where any particular theory belongs within it. Some reviews describe whole groups of theories – in particular, those deriving from welfare economics – as normative when they might more accurately be classed as positive. But if we accept that triad, I would argue that the main areas of possible relevance for geographers are the descriptive and the positive – particularly the latter. This is simply because they are the usual modes of theory-building in human geography. Ecological models of the city, or studies of the urban hierarchy, or the rank-size rule, are classical examples of descriptive theory. Central place theory and spatial interaction theory are standard examples of positive theory. The strengths and weaknesses of each are reasonably well known to all geographers.

From this, we can see that it is perfectly possible to 'believe in' both the rank-size rule and CPT at the same time. As table 3.3 shows, the differences between the models are so great that they do not contradict each other; they are complementary, and deal with different aspects of the urban system.

Table 3.3   Differences between central place theory and the rank-size distribution

	Rank-size	*CPT*
Scale	National	Regional
Approach	Inductive	Deductive
Theory	Descriptive	Positive

3.3   Central place theory: the spatial dimension

A major additional difference between the rank-size and CPT approaches – and indeed a major attraction of CPT for geographers – is that it also processes a spatial dimension. In simple terms, the hierarchy can also be identified as a particular pattern of settlements. Once more, the spatial dimension depends upon the operation of the two processes, the threshold, and the range of a good.

It is simplest if we regard the central place system developing chronologically. Let us begin with a landscape upon which there exists a series of small marketing settlements (figure 3.4(a)). To recap, these are spaced in order to fulfil the requirements of the shops' thresholds, and the willingness of consumers to travel (the range of the goods on offer within the settlements).

Around each settlement there is in effect a catchment area, although this of course assumes that consumers can travel equally in all directions, that populations are equally spaced and equally wealthy, and that retailers do not attempt to increase trade by reducing prices and increasing the range of their goods, in short, perfect competition is assumed. Given this, we expect a highly regular catchment system to evolve, as in figure 3.4(b). It will be noted that the catchments are hexagonal: this is to compensate for the poor 'packing' properties of circular catchments, and in other words a hexagonal lattice is the most efficient way to divide up space.

This is the beginning of the evolution of a full range of marketing functions. As we might now expect, higher order goods (those purchased less frequently, of higher cost) will only be available in a more limited number of settlements, due to the thresholds

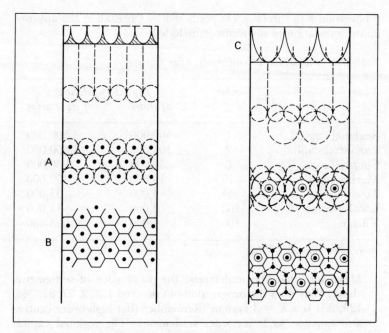

Figure 3.4 *a) Demand cones and their spatial arrangement*
b) Demand cones as hexagons to improve close packing
*c) The superimposition of demand cones for higher-order goods to
produce larger trade areas*

> *Note that this lattice assumes an isotropic surface, i.e. a flat plain with
> equal population distribution, no transportation problems and no
> physical barriers.*

involved. As a result, a second (and subsequent) layer(s) are added
to the lattice (figure 3.4(c)).

From figure 3.4, we get a glimpse of the way in which a CPT
landscape can be built up. The hexagonal arrangement means
that a certain level of settlement will always be found midway
between three larger settlements, and that any level of settlement
will always be surrounded by six centres of lesser importance.
These six settlements are themselves, of course, midway between
higher-order centres, which means that their populations do not
visit only one centre; in fact, their allegiance is spread across three
centres. Consequently, it is normal to assume that each centre of
a particular level is used by its own population, plus one-third of
each subsidiary's population. A simple calculation indicates why
this was termed a rule of three by Christaller $(1 + 6 \times 1/3 = 3)$;
using the German term Kreisstadt ('district town'), this is normally
known as a K = 3 SYSTEM. As we can see from table 3.4, a regular

progression – in threes – was predicted by Christaller; the approximate translation of his terms is included.

Table 3.4   Progression of settlements, after Christaller

Name	Number	Typical Population of centre	of trade areas
Regional capital	1	500,000	3,500,000
Provincial capital	2	100,000	1,000,000
County town	6	30,000	350,000
Market town	18	10,000	100,000
Town	54	4,000	35,000
Local centre	162	2,000	11,000
Village	486	1,000	3,500

Source: after Christaller, 1966

1. Make sure that you understand the progression of settlements above. Why does the progression not proceed 1, 3, 9, 27, 81, 243, 729, if it is a $K = 3$ system? Remember that high-order centres also function as lower-order settlements. The regional capital will also function as a provincial capital; consequently, there are not three provincial capitals, and neither are there nine county towns. There are however the *equivalents* of three provincial capitals, and nine county towns if the higher-order settlements are taken into account.

2. When was Christaller working and writing? What economic and social conditions will have changed since then which may have caused his population predictions to be an underestimate?

Discussion

When it comes to an evaluation of Christaller's work, we must be quite clear about his intentions. First and foremost, he wanted to devise a set of principles which would highlight the fundamental processes determining shopping behaviour within a region. Furthermore, his predictions concerning settlement sizes and patterns were based upon particular simplifying assumptions – such as the distribution of population and the ease of travel – in order to focus more clearly upon these processes rather than unique factors such as local geography or the quirks of history.

This approach has in the past been either misunderstood or simply rejected by some geographers, (Smailes 1971, p. 4):

Geography and history alike recognize the importance and rich

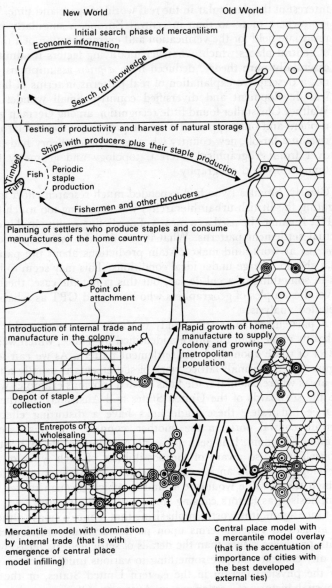

New World   Old World

Initial search phase of mercantilism
Economic information
Search for knowledge

Testing of productivity and harvest of natural storage
Ships with producers plus their staple production
Timber
Fish   Periodic
Furs   staple
production
Fishermen and other producers

Planting of settlers who produce staples and consume manufactures of the home country
Point of attachment

Introduction of internal trade and manufacture in the colony
Rapid growth of home manufacture to supply colony and growing metropolitan population
Depot of staple collection

Entrepots of wholesaling

Mercantile model with domination by internal trade (that is with emergence of central place model infilling)

Central place model with a mercantile model overlay (that is the accentuation of importance of cities with the best developed external ties)

Figure 3.5   The development of variations in the basic CPT model. Through the various stages of the diagram, a CPT lattice in the Old World (e.g. Britain) is altered by trading links with a New World Seaboard (on the left of the diagram). These mercantile links are superimposed upon the usual central places in both countries (after Vance, 1970).

interest of the particular in the real world of space and time. This is nowhere more so than in central Europe, a singularly inappropriate field for the verification and exemplification of a theory of central places which, whatever modifying factors it admits, is essentially pure theory, deduced from *a priori* assumptions, and not a descriptive explanation of real patterns in terms of historical development and diversified country. Small wonder that Walther Christaller found little recognition among German geographers and only appeared a major prophet among social theorists in a far-off, new country when concern for theory had taken over from geographical interest, topology and geometry from topography and geography.

Clearly, Smailes (who had expended much research effort investigating the British urban hierarchy) was expecting too much from CPT. It cannot be used as a means of predicting reality: in this case, actual settlement patterns. What it can do is to isolate particular *processes* at work, and make certain predictions about the patterns that should emerge under ideal conditions. This may seem to leave us in something of a cul-de-sac, but this is not the case; there are several examples of geographers who have used CPT as a basis for detailed analysis.

A particularly interesting study is Vance's *mercantile model*. This takes its name from the process identified by Vance, which was the effect of trade upon the basic settlement pattern. As we can see in figure 3.5, a 'normal' lattice work of settlements is usually altered in areas where colonial trade links existed (obvious examples would be the seaboards of the United States and Australia). Further, as Vance illustrates, these trade links have a distorting effect on certain coastal ports in the 'mother' country – in this case the United Kingdom. It is perhaps worth pointing out that Christaller himself was also aware of the possibilities of such types of links developing, and in an alternative scheme, he drew up a lattice in which the K value would be 4, and in which through routes were emphasised as factors causing some settlements to grow.

Once again, it is worth emphasising that Vance's study, although it focuses in general terms upon particular situations, is dealing with processes rather than the details of settlement patterns, which in any context will owe something to various unique factors, such as the physical terrain in the eastern United States, or the very unusual history of settlement in Australia. Of course, there are many situations in which geographers are interested in the detailed study of particular settlements, and in these cases, rather different research strategies are necessary, although CPT still provides the basic framework. We will turn to these in the next chapter.

Key issues

HIERARCHY See 'Key Issues' to chapter 2. To summarize the significance of the hierarchy in settlement geography we can say:
1. Settlements, as retail and service centres, have an organisational structure – with the largest city at the top providing the most specialised services and the base of the hierarchy being occupied by the very numerous small settlements providing the bare minimum of services, or even none at all.
2. Given the right conditions – an isotropic plain with an even population spread – the structural organisation that emerges will give rise to a spatial pattern of organisation as described by CPT.

CENTRAL PLACE THEORY (CPT) A geographic theory dealing with settlements as service centres ('central places'). Its chief significance is its explanatory power; it has helped our understanding and explanation of the structural and spatial organisation of settlements, and the relationship between settlements of different sizes. It does this by isolating the processes by which services are supplied to people. The two fundamental ideas are the threshold and the range of goods.

THRESHOLD Very simply, we can see that for a retail business to succeed a certain minimum level of custom is required. This gives us the threshold population of the service and, of course, the actual figure for a particular business depends on the nature of that business. A high threshold is required for the very specialised type of shop which might only have one potential customer per 100 population. A general store or sub-post office requires a lower threshold population; we all need bread and post office facilities on a regular basis.

THE RANGE OF A GOOD Clearly, people living in a region are to a greater or lesser degree mobile (see Book 2, *Interaction*, Chapter 1). They are able to travel in order to obtain goods and services. The distance people are willing to travel to obtain a particular good depends on the good; obviously not too far for a loaf of bread, but a greater distance for a specialised article of sports equipment or a piece of furniture. Thus, the more specialised the good, the greater its 'range' (and the higher up the hierarchy a central place is, the greater its service area).

SPATIAL SCALE As in many fields of geography, the size of the area under study is an important consideration in settlement geography. It is important to bear in mind that whereas the rank-size rule is a regularity often to be found in whole nations, CPT is a theory developed not for whole nations or continents, but for smaller regions.

K-SYSTEMS Christaller assumed that settlement patterns would conform to 'fixed k' patterns – $k = 3$, $k = 4$ or $k = 7$ – that is, very predictable mathematical progressions of settlements of different sizes would emerge. An alternative view was developed by August Lösch (pronounced 'Lersh'), who suggested that far more complicated (variable k) systems could develop: see, for example, Bradford and Kent, 1977).

4
Central place theory and the real world

4.1 Applying CPT

We have seen that CPT has had its critics. As Ross Davies shows below, these criticisms may be based on misapprehensions ('a negative type of criticism') or overexpectations ('those who have tended to claim too much'). Davies himself however shows that there are real weaknesses, but despite these the theory provides a good starting point for different types of investigation (1976, pp. 28–29):

> There has been considerable support both for and against the overall effectiveness of central place theory in explaining the locational relationships of centres and their trade areas. Unfortunately, much of the serious debate about its relevance has been coloured by a negative type of criticism which rejects outright the appropriateness of any high degree of abstraction for dealing with the real world. This criticism focuses particularly on the assumptions made about underlying isotropic conditions and the rational economic behaviour of consumers. Against this, there have been others who have tended to claim too much for the theory and who have taken it beyond its original limited intentions. Specifically, this has occurred when the theory has been used to provide a general explanation for the sizes and spacing of all settlements (or alternatively all shopping centres inside cities) regardless of the extent to which they actually function as central places or not.
>
> The main weaknesses of the theory are that it is extremely rigid and deterministic and that it describes a mainly static set of locational relationships. It refers exclusively to a range of business and related service activities that respond to the single process of centralisation and, within the context of real world situations, it is difficult to distinguish these from other activities which reflect much more on agglomerative and other forces. This inability to properly differentiate centralised versus non-centralised activities consequently means that it is virtually impossible to verify precise specifications about frequencies of centres and

networks of trade areas without substantial statistical analyses and data transformations. Likewise, there are no summary mathematical formulae which can be easily manipulated and adapted to suit local conditions on the ground, for those models which have been formulated usually assume that a fixed K proportionality factor can be empirically derived. Any forecasting or projection of the size relationships of centres in practical terms has therefore to be accomplished by other means (mainly regression analysis).

In contrast to these limitations, the broader notions of the theory, particularly the hierarchy construct, have given extremely useful terms of reference and organisational concepts within which to examine systematic regularities in settlements and shopping centres. Indeed, many studies have utilised the hierarchy construct with little conscious reference to the theory that surrounds it. The main purpose has been to provide a general classification of size orders within which individual settlements and/or shopping centres may be more consistently compared. Such studies have either been descriptive of the actual states of a system at any one time, or alternatively they have been prescriptive of optimum states to be realised in the future.

Discussion

Davies makes several points, and it is worthwhile identifying these clearly. First, he is critical of those who attempt to force *all* settlements into a CPT framework; as Vance's work shows, other forces exist. Second, he points out that CPT assumes only one process, namely shopping behaviour leading to the centralisation of retailing. As he goes on to say however, other forces do exist within the urban system. He identified, for example, AGGLOMERATION, or the tendency for certain functions to cluster together – an obvious example would be the way in which educational institutions like universities, polytechnics and colleges may all be located close together, which in turn will stimulate demand for bookshops, catering and many other service facilities.

Because of this limitation, he argues that it is virtually impossible to predict the exact size and layout of any regional hierarchy. Nonetheless his evaluation is generally favourable, and as he notes, the very basic notion of a hierarchy has been a useful starting point for many researchers and planners.

4.2 A shopping hierarchy investigated

The following example builds upon Davis' remarks concerning the use of the general principles of CPT: 'many studies have utilised the hierarchy construct with little conscious reference to the theory that surrounds it'. It is an empirical investigation of the retailing structure in an 800 km^2 area surrounding York. As a measure of the centrality of each settlement, a very simple statistic has been used, namely the total retail shop frontage. Most studies employ the floor area of the shops in each settlement (measured in square metres or square feet) but frontage is easier to collect and may be crudely measured by pacing the length of each shop front. The data collected are shown in table 4.1.

Table 4.1 Totals of shop frontage, York area

Centre	Shop frontage	Total population
York	3,922	106,000
Selby	1,205	11,340
Malton	958	4,190
Thirsk	527	3,500
Pocklington	403	3,980
Tadcaster	267	5,103
Boroughbridge	199	1,950
Sherburne in Elmet	111	2,776
Easingwold	91	2,686
Cawood	79	967
Riccall	44	783
Sheriff Hutton	26	615
Brayton	22	1,061
Thorpe Willoughby	21	292
South Milford	16	1,042
Elvington	15	386
Terrington	14	350
Rufforth	14	265
Healaugh	10	225
Wheldrake	9	451
Green Hammerton	9	497
Tollerton	8	513
Leavingham	6	225
Newton	6	371
Thorganby	6	278
Acklam	3	145

1. Referring to figure 4.1 for an example of the scales and axes, transfer the data from table 4.1 to graph paper. Remember that both axes are in logarithmic form.

2. Examine your graph and in concise terms describe the relation-

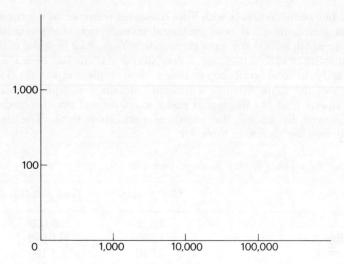

*Figure 4.1   Logarithmic axes for plotting population and frontage data. See text
for details*

ship between population size and centrality, as measured by
shop frontage. We suggest that if more precise measures of
association are required, RANK CORRELATIONS should be used.

3. Examine your graph in more detail and, paying close attention
to both variables, attempt to group the settlements by drawing
a short dividing line between groups on the graph. We suggest
that the data fall naturally into four groups; York is clearly the
major centre, and at the other end of the scale there are
numerous villages. Can you also identify what we might term
'small towns' and a 'market town'. (The population sizes used
in table 3.4 may be useful here, although you should not expect
too close a correlation.)

Discussion

What you have identified from these data is of course a *settlement
hierarchy*. As CPT predicts for us, settlements functioning as central
places tend to form distinct population groups – each group being
a separate level within the hierarchy. The specific dividing lines
that you have drawn on the graph represent the thresholds of the
different goods that they each offer, which is shown more clearly
if we examine in addition table 4.2

In table 4.2, we can see that four different types of good have
been identified. All the settlements offer food shops; the small towns
possess shops selling some types of clothes, the market town has
some chain stores (although this is not clear from the data above),

and the largest centre, York, has a large range of specialist shops. This information is of course entirely consistent with what we noted in Chapter 3 and CPT gives us the key that enables us to interpret the figures quite easily. What we can identify in table 4.2 are the *thresholds* for the four different types of retailing activity; food shops, clothing shops, multiple household stores and specialist shops.

Table 4.2 Settlements and floorspace, York area A = food shops; B = clothing, C = household goods D = specialist services (antiques, books etc.)

Centre: population	Floorspace:	A	B	C	D
York	106,000	592	1,272	805	1,253
Selby	11,340	352	266	533	54
Tadcaster	5,103	88	47	65	67
Malton	4,190	192	333	353	80
Pocklington	3,980	94	139	168	32
Thirsk	3,500	137	122	242	26
Sherburne-in-Elmet	2,776	62	35	14	—
Easingwold	2,686	34	22	31	4
Boroughbridge	1,950	75	21	73	30
Brayton	1,061	22	—	—	—
South Milford	1,042	16	—	—	—
Cawood	967	57	—	18	4
Riccall	783	24	—	19	—
Sheriff Hutton	615	26	—	—	—
Tollerton	513	8	—	—	—
Green Hammerton	497	9	—	—	—
Wheldrake	451	9	—	—	—
Elvington	386	15	—	—	—
Newton	371	6	—	—	—
Terrington	350	14	—	—	—
Thorpe Will'by	292	21	—	—	—
Thorganby	278	6	—	—	—
Rufforth	265	14	—	—	—
Healaugh	225	10	—	—	—
Leavingham	225	6	—	—	—
Acklam	145	3	—	—	—

Coda

In this short example, we have used CPT to reveal the underlying structure of retail provision in a small region. For simplicity's sake,

we have focused upon a small area, without the 'distractions' of
large-scale industry or major topographic changes. Certainly, some
further empirical investigation of, for example, the *range* of different
goods and SERVICES is useful, as this shows the spatial extent of
the trade areas of different settlements, and two examples of this
are illustrated in figure 4.2. (A fuller discussion is given in chapter
8 of Everson and Fitzgerald, 1969.)

What we have *not* done is to investigate the *patterns* of settlement
within this area from a CPT perspective; we have not attempted
to find a rigid, hexagonal lattice. In our view, the geometric
outcomes of Christaller's ideas are probably the least significant
and the most abstract part of his model. We would not expect a
hexagonal landscape of settlements to emerge in the real world,
although attempts have been made to find them (see again Everson

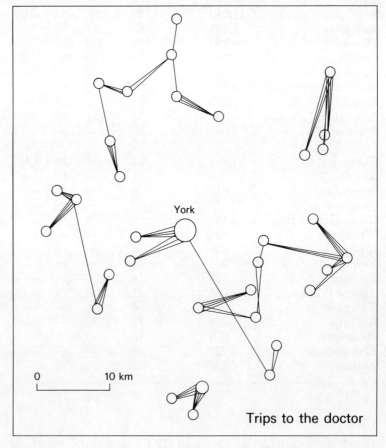

Figure 4.2   a) Trade areas around York for doctors' surgeries

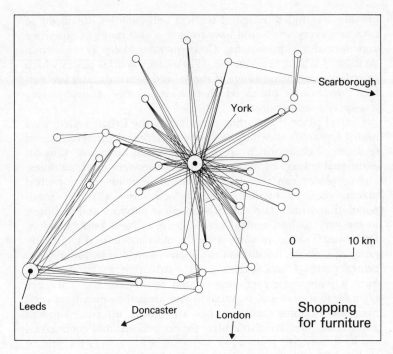

b) Trade areas around York for household goods

and Fitzgerald, 1969, pp. 77–100). As we shall see in section 4.4, the
lattice is far more useful when used to plan and provide services from
scratch. (Also see photographic section.)

4.3 A service hierarchy investigated

It is not only in the fields of retailing that CPT has provided an
intellectual framework for research. The political scientist Professor
Ken Newton has drawn on Christaller's ideas to investigate levels
of *service* provision in cities. He writes (1981, pp. 119–20):

> There is one well-developed body of work about systems of cities
> which may serve as a starting point for the explanation of urban
> spending patterns, and this is the work of geographers on
> central place theory and the urban hierarchy. At the heart of
> this work is the idea that urban places exist to provide services
> and facilities not only for their own residents, but also for the
> populations of their hinterlands. Thus: 'one of the main functions
> of a town – or any service centre – is to supply the needs of the
> population around it'. Clearly it is impossible for all cities to

provide a complete range of services and facilities, for to do so each and every one would have to have a vast range of expensive and specialised provisions. Consequently, there is an urban division of labour between the highest-order central places which cater for an extensive range of specialized demands, and successively lower-order places which provide a range of successively less-specialized services.

Central place theory thus conceives of the urban system as a nested hierarchy in which each city provides all the services and facilities of cities which are below it in the hierarchy, plus an additional range of more specialized services and facilities. Urban places can therefore be ranked from low-order central places, such as market towns, which serve a rather small population with a fairly narrow range of services and facilities, to the very highest central places, such as New York, London, Paris, and Tokyo, which provide the most specialized and costly range of services, in addition to all those provided by lower-order central places. Cities at the top of the urban hierarchy, therefore, have a wide variety of inter-related characteristics. They are often large in terms of population and area: they provide a wide range of shopping facilities; they are centres for entertainment and leisure, they are also centres for professional and commercial services; they are regional or national headquarters for private and public organizations such as banks, insurance companies, chain stores, trade unions, professional, business, and voluntary organisations, they are often government centres; and lastly, because they are centres of business and pleasure, they attract large numbers of commuters and visitors.

But what does all this have to do with the public expenditure of city governments? The answer is that a city's position in the urban hierarchy may affect its public expenditure in two main ways. First, city governments are themselves likely to provide a range of specialized services in accordance with their city's importance as a central place. High order central places are likely to have large and specialized municipal cultural centres, an extensive range of parks and recreational facilities, and a variety of specialized schools and educational institutions. To this extent, it might be hypothesised that the higher the city ranks in the central place hierarchy the more it is likely to spend on the public services which form part of the city's function as a service centre. While central place theory was initially developed by economists and geographers in order to explain the distribution of private sector facilities and services, it may be possible to adopt the theory to explain the distribution of some public-sector services as well.

Secondly, the higher a city's rank in the urban hierarchy, the more likely it is to attract commuters and visitors who make demands upon public services. Planning and maintaining a clean and effective road and public transport system is likely to be expensive, the public health standards of private hotels and restaurants, and of public facilities, will have to be maintained, large quantities of litter and refuse will have to be moved, parks and open spaces will have to be provided, and large crowds and population movements will have to be regulated. Consequently, the more important the central place, the more it is likely to have to spend on roads, public transports, public health, parks, refuse, and police.

Newton's study uses correlation tests to examine the relationship between levels of public service provision and centrality, and he concludes (1981, p. 131) that:

Central place theory, it is argued, is relevant to public spending ... the higher a city's place in the urban hierarchy, the greater its per capita expenditures on these services is likely to be.

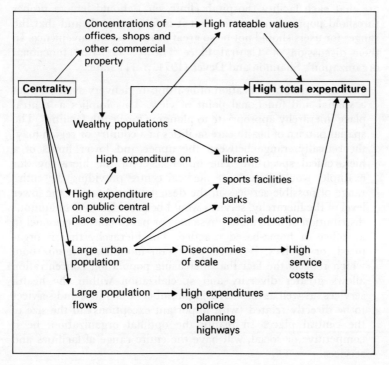

Figure 4.3   A causal model relating centrality and local public expenditure
(Source: *Newton, 1981*)

As figure 4.3 shows, it is possible to develop a relatively complicated flow diagram to explain this link in detail. This work is
interesting, therefore, for two reasons. First, because it shows
another context within which CPT has explicitly provided an
inspiration to practical research, and second, because it provides
another dimension to our understanding of the cities in which we
live. In addition to our emphasis upon the daily urban system and
retailing provision, we must also now view cities as locations in
which services are concentrated for both residents and those in
surrounding settlements.

4.4 The provision of medical facilities

As we noted above, CPT has also been employed as an ideal system
of organisation when services are being designed. This is in keeping
with Hall's remarks (see in Chapter 3) concerning CPT as a
normative theory, that is, dealing with what *should* happen. In the
case of the design of, for example, health care facilities, the 'norms'
are that each facility (hospital, clinic, etc.) should have a proper
threshold population (that is, that it is fully utilised) and that the
ranges for users should not be so great as to cause inconvenience. In
their discussion of 'Central Place Theory: a spatial functional
organization', Shannon and Dever (1974, p. 11) state:

> One may view organization of health care delivery systems from
> a spatial and functional point of view. This implies a 'central
> place' hierarchy appropriate to planning for health facilities. The
> spatial pattern of health care facilities in a country or region may,
> theoretically, range between the upper and lower limits of a
> hierarchical spectrum. The upper level of the hierarchy, for
> example, would be a large medical centre providing the entire
> range of possible services in the designated region. At the lower
> level of the hierarchy, services would be provided by a ubiquitous
> distribution of individual physicians or paramedical personnel in
> an office or home-based practice. The hierarchy that is orga-
> nized, or evolves, is based partly on functional organization,
> which reflects the fact that increasing population concentration
> allows greater diversity and specialization within the health
> services, as well as an increasing number of facilities and services
> to be directly related (with important exceptions) to the size of
> the central place. In reality the optimal organization, be it
> competitive or social, will have the entire range of facilities and
> services.

As figure 4.4 indicates, the ideal organization of a health system
is explicitly reminiscent of a CPT lattice work. As the authors note,

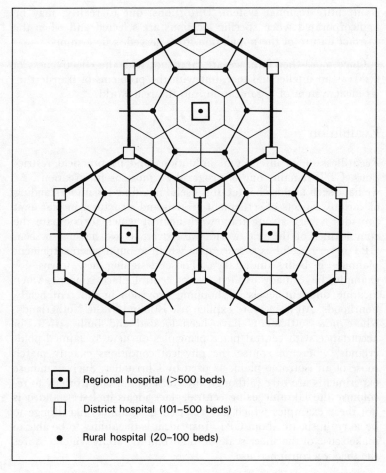

Figure 4.4   A theoretical organisation of a local health service, using central place principles

however, these norms are sometimes difficult to achieve because of local geographical factors (1974, p. 11):

> The spatial organization is more difficult to realize because of many irregularities in the region. Such irregularities include localized resources, variation in population densities, a hierarchical transportation network, and other peculiar cultural and physical constraints that spatially distort attempts to optimize facility patterns and service areas based on theoretical considerations of an isotropic plain. Nevertheless, when health care planning decisions are being made, it is useful to think first of the 'ideal' (functional and spatial) hierarchy and location pattern for

an entire regional system. Distortions, due to reality, may be incorporated when specific locations are selected and when the exact nature of the population to be served is determined.

Once more therefore, we are faced not with the effectiveness of CPT as an intellectual tool, but with the problems of transferring its ideal system of organization into the real world.

4.5 Evaluation

Regardless of its intellectual limitations and its practical restrictions, CPT remains one of geography's most useful creations. As we have seen in this chapter, it is useful in aiding the understanding of various aspects of settlement growth and structure, insofar as it provides a very strong framework against which to compare the complexities of the real world. Moreover, as we have also seen, CPT is very useful as a basis upon which to build when settlement planning is being undertaken. Those designing new towns, for example, have made explicit use of central place concepts when locating different levels of shopping provision in different neighbourhoods. An even more explicit use is found in the Netherlands, where new settlements have been located and built strictly in accordance with central place principles on new, reclaimed polderlands, where of course the physical conditions exactly match those of an isotropic plain, as used by Christaller. Such grandiose experiments are rare (although the Nazis did attempt briefly to recolonise the Ukraine using central place ideals in 1944), and it is not these examples which have caused geographers like Bunge to be so enthusiastic about CPT. Instead, it is the ability to be able to make sense of the sheer scale of the urban hierarchy which ensures the theory's continued use.

Key Issues

AGGLOMERATION AND AGGLOMERATIVE FORCES Agglomeration implies the massing together of economic activities (types of industrial and service activities) at the same location. The forces of agglomeration, therefore, refer to the processes that lead to agglomeration. More specifically, there are distinct advantages, that can be measured in economic terms, to be gained by firms or businesses locating near each other. The significance of agglomeration in the context of CPT is that it is an additional process not really taken account of by the theory in its initial form. In other words, we might expect that a pattern predicted by CPT could well be distorted by the forces of agglomeration.

RANK CORRELATION Spearman's rank correlation coefficient is probably the most straightforward method of calculating the strength of a relationship between two sets of data. For the technique, refer to a text such as '*Science in Geography*', 4 (McCullagh 1974). For present purposes we should simply remember that the strength of the statistical relationship is measured on a scale from $-1 \to 0 \to +1$, 0 indicating absolutely no statistical connection between the two sets of data, and -1 and $+1$ indicating a perfect negative and positive relationship respectively. The nearer to ± 1 the coefficient is, the stronger the statistical relationship.

SERVICES We usually think of services or service industries as 'tertiary activity' to distinguish it from 'primary' (mining, etc.) and 'secondary' (manufacturing) activities. There are, of course, many categories of service industries; retailing (Christaller's main concern) is one. Distinct from retailing, but still service activities, are the various *public services* such as health and education provided by government (sometimes local or sometimes national government. See Book 1, *The Region*, for a discussion on local authority areas; information on the actual services provided by the different local authority areas can be found elsewhere, (for example, Lambert, 1981).

5
Conclusion: in search of the good city

5.1 Alternative ways of looking at cities

Throughout this book, we have simply looked at settlements as collections of people; we have considered the city as a daily urban system, and as a marketing settlement (it can of course be both at once). So far, however, we have said very little about whether urbanisation is a 'good' thing or even a normal phenomenon. Much of the literature on urban growth in the developing world uses indicators – such as the number of 'millionaire cities' – as some measurement of progress and development; this is, however, to adopt a culturally-biased view of the urbanisation process, and one that lacks historical depth. Any nineteenth-century text indicates the appalling standards of living that accompanied rapid urban growth in Europe, and we are witnessing a replication of poor conditions in Cairo, Calcutta and São Paulo today. Let us not become so involved with our examination of cities, therefore, that we overlook the problems that can exist there, and the variations in the quality of life between one settlement and another.

In Book 1, we examined the variations in a level of living index for Great Britain as a whole, and we saw that it is possible to differentiate between areas (in this case, counties) in terms of various measures like unemployment and mortality. We can do something similiar for individual towns, although different approaches are possible.

For example, in figure 5.1 we have a diagram which indicates the variations that exist in terms of housing tenure between towns. We shall be discussing housing in greater detail in Book 4, *The City*, but in very simple terms we can say that owner-occupied housing is relatively expensive, and that privately-rented accommodation is often old and of poor quality; council housing is relatively cheap, but usually of a high standard, although difficult to enter unless a family has had its name on a waiting list for some time.

When we examine figure 5.1, we can immediately differentiate between various types of town. Aim to find examples in each case:

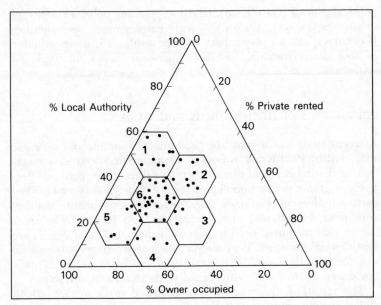

(*Source*: Robson, 1979)

Figure 5.1   *Patterns of tenure, 1971. Towns with populations ≥ 100,000 in 1971 are shown. They are grouped into 6 crude classes shown in the numbered hexagons which combine varying proportions of the three tenures.*

Group 1:   Basildon, Dudley, Sunderland, Thurrock, Walsall, Warley, West Bromwich, Wolverhampton.

Group 2:   Hull, Liverpool, Manchester, Newcastle, Norwich, Nottingham, Salford, Sheffield, South Shields.

Group 3:   Brighton, Greater London, Oxford.

Group 4:   Bournemouth, Southend, Torbay.

Group 5:   Blackburn, Blackpool, Bolton, Luton, Nottingham, Poole, Solihull.

Group 6:   Birkenhead, Birmingham, Bradford, Bristol, Cardiff, Coventry, Derby, Havant & Waterloo, Huddersfield, Ipswich, Leeds, Leicester, Newport, Oldham, Plymouth, Portsmouth, Reading, St. Helens, Southampton, Stockport, Stoke, Swansea, Teesside, York.

1. Those with high amounts of private renting and owner-occupation: this implies an expensive town.
2. Those with little other than owner-occupied housing: an over-spill or suburban settlement.
3. Those with large proportions of council housing: cheap accommodation, but often as a result of high unemployment and low incomes.

Of course, it is very difficult to infer anything systematic from one variable such as housing. The tenure groups in figure 5.1 owe their development to many factors interacting over a long period;

political control (Gateshead), land-use planning policies restricting urban expansion (Oxford), local employment opportunities (Coventry), can all play a part. Consequently, it is more valuable to look for systematic variations between towns, or types of settlement.

5.2   An analysis of British towns and cities

A recent study has sought 'the good city'. In an analysis very like that used by Paul Knox in Book 1, Donnison and Soto have investigated the standards of life in 154 towns throughout Britain, effectively, all those with a population greater than 50,000 people. They used 40 different variables, measuring unemployment, housing conditions, educational attainment, race and income. The techniques that they used need not detain us here, but their results are fairly straightforward. Very simply, they used 'cluster analysis' to put together the towns that were most similar in terms of their 'goodness' or 'badness' with regard to these sorts of variables.

The results of the study are summarised in figure 5.2, which shows the distribution of types of cluster; each one is discussed briefly in table 5.1.

On the basis of their analysis, Donnison and Soto identify a sharp contrast between what they term 'new Britain' and 'traditional Britain'. As we can see from table 5.1, traditional Britain contains the declining settlements – those which are losing their industrial base and their wealth, and which are in consequence becoming settlements in which various types of deprivation are becoming concentrated. (This process is of course the relative decline of some types of settlements that we noted in Chapter 2, table 2.3). New Britain, on the other hand, contains the settlements which are prospering, in which unemployment is below the national average, and in which the new industries and services are concentrated. Again, as table 5.1 shows, it is here that the good life is to be found.

1. Make a list of the types of settlements that constitute 'traditional Britain'. What do they have in common? (Figure 5.1 is useful here.) How long have they been in decline? What are the prospects of a recovery for these settlements? (It may be valuable to examine how long some of these towns have been receiving government assistance; see Book 1.)

2. Make a list of the types of settlements that consitute 'new Britain', and again, using figure 5.1, suggest what they have in common. Have these towns grown naturally or has their expansion been planned? (A glance at sections 1.3 and 1.4 should be useful.)

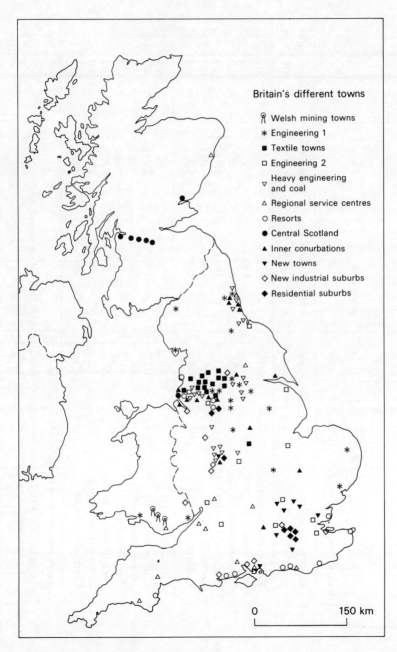

Figure 5.2   The distribution of types of cluster

Table 5.1   Urban clusters with statistical descriptions*

Clusters/variables	Households owning a car	Households with all amenities†	Unemployed	Workers with A-levels
New Britain				
Residential suburbs	269	117	49	167
New towns	179	119	57	124
New industrial suburbs	159	111	63	109
Regional Service Centres	97	101	100	124
London	114	96	76	121
Resorts	108	107	106	97
Traditional Britain				
Engineering (I)	83	99	89	81
Engineering (II)	102	106	100	83
Heavy engineering	78	102	94	63
Textile towns	71	93	93	72
Welsh mining towns	51	69	122	62
Inner conurbations	62	95	147	69
Central Scotland	40	101	205	145

Source: extracted from Donnison and Soto, 1980

* Data for 1971: 100 represents the national average throughout the 154 towns analysed.
† Homes possessing exclusive use of washing facilities and WCs.

CLUSTERS	Examples	CLUSTERS	Examples	CLUSTERS	Examples
Residential suburbs	Cheadle; Epsom; Solihull	Resorts	Torbay; Hove; Southend	Welsh mining towns	Aberdare; Merthyr; Rhondda
New towns	Harlow; Stevenage; East Kilbride	Engineering (I)	Carlisle; Derby; Ipswich; Swansea	Inner conurbations	Gateshead; Manchester; Leeds
New industrial suburbs	Poole; Watford; Pudsey	Engineering (II)	Luton; Grimsby; Swindon	Central Scotland	Dundee; Motherwell; Paisley; Glasgow
Regional service centre	Reading; Exeter; Bristol Oxford	Heavy engineering	Jarrow; Barnsley; Wigan		
London	London and Cambridge	Textile towns	Blackburn; Bolton; Halifax		

3. Donnison and Soto's research seems to suggest that there are some very specific trends at work within the British urban system, and their findings fit in with the data presented in Chapter 1. What do you expect might happen to the urban hierarchy in Britain in future decades? Do you think the growth of the planned settlements will be at the expense of the old conurbations, with the result that the rank-size distribution may change? Or will the graph maintain its historical stability? (See figure 2.5.)

5.3 For and against large cities

One of the consistent themes to emerge in this volume is the decline of the large city in Britain. Although the evidence from the United States and Britain shows that ever greater expanses are being covered in concrete, it would be wrong to infer that people like living in big settlements. Quite the reverse. Urban sprawl occurs because people want to leave the conurbations, and the built-up area expands as the outer suburbs and small dormitory towns themselves expand.

Although economists have heatedly debated what is the 'optimum' city size – measured in terms of the costs of providing services like public transport, hospitals and sewers – it seems that urban populations have reached their own conclusions, and voted with their feet. Their decisions are not based entirely upon economic criteria, although it is clear that life in big cities *can* be

Table 5.2   Crime rates and city size, United Kingdom 1965

Population	No. of areas	No. of crimes per 100,000 pop.	Serious crimes per 100,000 pop.
London	1	3,378	1,565
Cities >400,000	6	3,327	1,365
Large towns >200,000	11	3,333	867
Medium towns >100,000	29	2,795	741
Small towns <100,000	27	2,544	584
County areas	50	1,747	510

Source: extracted from Richardson, 1973

Table 5.3   Crimes rates and city size, United States 1970

Population	No. of areas	No. of crimes per 100,000	Violent crimes per 100,000
>250,000	58	6,485	860
>100,000	97	5,116	359
>50,000	265	4,058	232
>25,000	462	3,401	174
>10,000	1,233	2,893	136
<10,000	2,202	2,327	109
'Suburbs'	2,341	2,904	163
Rural areas	1,620	1,266	103

very expensive. Far more important are the *social* costs, the externalities (in the sense that we used the term in Book 2). Again, the evidence from both the United Kingdom and the United States is that large cities are unhealthy (due to smog and pollution) and even dangerous. Tables 5.2 and 5.3 show some comparative statistics for crime rates on both sides of the Atlantic, measured in terms of city size.

Of course, there is no automatic relationship between conurbations and crime, although a large population does of course increase the opportunities for a wider variety of crime and reduces the chances of detection. Similarly, some sorts of crime are more rigorously pursued in large cities; drug offences might be an example. Nonetheless, these figures are commonly perceived to be correct by residents, and it is this perception which has produced dissatisfaction and suburban drift, as figure 5.2 shows. It should be emphasised that these migrants do not seek a rural existence, they do not want to cut themselves off entirely from the schools, hospitals and other services available within a built-up area. Indeed, it is a common complaint in the United States that these households act as 'free loaders', in that they live cheaply in the prosperous suburbs, but still use the entertainment and other services in the adjacent cities without paying for them through local property taxes, the American equivalent of *rates* in the United Kingdom. (See Book 2, figure 2.1.) Moreover, suburban drift reveals more sharply the unemployment, deprivation and sense of crisis for those remaining within the large cities. This is not a problem which is likely to be solved easily, despite the seriousness of the malaise, as witnessed by riots in the United States in the 1960s and 1970s, and in Britain in the 1980s.

Photographic section

1 A satellite's view of S. E. England

This photograph, taken by Landsat in July 1979, shows much of general geographical interest and time may usefully be spent studying the photograph with the help of an atlas map of the same region.

1. Identify the main urban areas within S. E. England. As well as Greater London itself you should easily find Cambridge, Luton, Ipswich and Brighton. It may also be possible to find major features within Greater London, notably Heathrow airport and the Lea Valley.

2. It is not difficult from this photograph to imagine the uncontrolled and relentless outward spread of Greater London during the inter-war period, and the alarm it caused geographers and planners at the time. Remind yourself of the planning legislation introduced after the Second World War; you should be able to relate this to the photograph by identifying several of the 'first generation' New Towns around London.

3. The pressure of urban expansion continued unabated into the 1960s which led to even more radical New Town proposals – the creation of larger planned settlements at greater distances from London. Is it possible to identify Northampton, Milton Keynes and Peterborough on this photograph?

A photograph is literally a 'snapshot', a moment in time. However, the photograph here cannot conceal from the imaginative student the changes constantly occurring to the urban system in S. E. England.

2 Courage Brewery, Reading, Berkshire

This aerial photograph was taken in 1977, facing south. In the foreground can be seen a major construction site, on which a new brewery has been erected.

1. The old Courage brewery is located in the centre of Reading. Why has the new site been chosen on the edge of the town on a greenfield site?

2. What do you imagine will happen to the old brewery site when it is ultimately demolished?

This example is useful because it emphasises that 'new Britain' is not entirely to do with office developments and research establishments. Many of the settlements in this category identified in Chapter 5 are dependent on light engineering and distributional activity. The M4 corridor and the still-expanding Heathrow airport complex are obvious examples of this, with towns like Reading and Slough employing quite large numbers of blue collar workers.

3 Traditional Britain: Mortimore Street, Consett

This scene was photographed early in 1982, in a town which in 1980 lost its only major source of employment, the British Steel Corporation plant. Not all of the town looks like this, but many residents are leaving the area, and as other smaller businesses also fold up, the future does not look encouraging.

1. The photograph shows a street of houses; in what decade were they built? What amenities are they likely to lack?

2. The juxtaposition of town and slag-heap is a typical perception of Northern towns, and one that deters industrialists. Examine a map of the North East, and identify nearby settlements which are having more success than Consett in attracting new industrial investment.

3. Urban geography cannot be understood without reference to other issues. Why was a steelworks built in Consett in the nineteenth century, and why did it close in the twentieth?

4. Should Consett be allowed to fade away, or should it, like Corby (see photograph 4, Book I), have public investment lavished upon it? How would you spend public money to improve this kind of scene?

4 Reclaimed Polderlands, Netherlands

This aerial picture shows productive farmland reclaimed from the sea. The fact that the settlement and transport pattern was established artificially means that enormous regularity has been created; all the roads are straight, all the fields are the same area, and all the farmsteads are regularly located. With such precision, we would expect the settlement pattern as a whole (hamlets, towns and villages) to be equally predictable, although the complexity of the decision-making that lies behind the location of a service and retail centre means that a device like central place theory is particularly important.

5 Virgin Megastore, Oxford Street, London

This picture shows the exterior of one of the large independent record shops established by Richard Branson in the 1970s. Before this time, large stores dealing exclusively with modern music and its impedimenta (cassettes, videos, posters, badges, books and personal appearances) were virtually unknown. However, the need to distribute in bulk and the rapid obsolescence of stock means that large economies of scale are necessary. In other words, large shops are necessary for profit, and in turn, a large threshold is required. Virgin stores are only found in large centres, like Manchester, Newcastle, Southampton.

1. Can you foresee any circumstances in which such stores would require a smaller threshold, and could then be located in smaller settlements?

6 The fall of Saigon

This dramatic picture shows the scenes of panic that ensued as it was realised that the Americans were about to leave Saigon in the face of the final North Vietnamese offensive in 1975. (See also photograph 4, Book 2).

The Viet Cong success came at the end of three decades of warfare, during which the North Vietnamese attempted to recapture the south of the country from first French, and latterly American forces. The length of time this took however meant that both countries evolved quite separately, with very different economies, styles of life and urban systems. The fall of Saigon – now renamed Ho Chi Minh City – has initiated the creation of a new urban system, which is simply a rough amalgamation of the formerly separate parts.

1. What has happened to the separate components within the new state of Vietnam? Which settlements have lost population (see, for example, the *Geographical Digest*, post-1975)

2. Is there any tendency for a rank-size distribution to emerge within the new urban system?

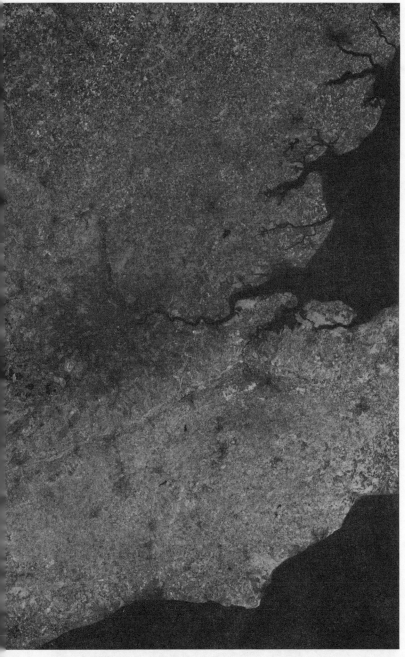

Photograph 1   A satellite's view of S. E. England

Photograph 2 Courage Brewery, Reading, Berkshire

Photograph 3   Traditional Britain: Mortimore Street, Consett

Photograph 4   Reclaimed Polderlands, Netherlands

Photograph 5   Virgin Megastore, Oxford Street, London

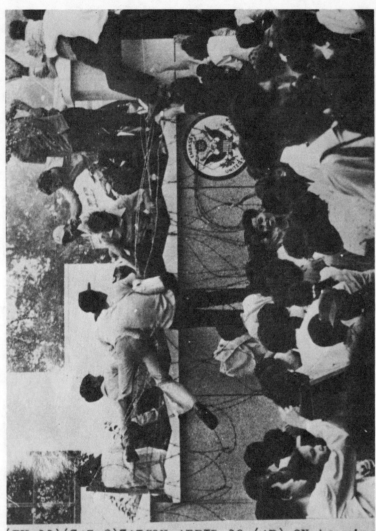

(BK-33)(SAI-2)SAIGON,APRIL 30-(AP)-ON hearing
of the Americans final evacuation, screaming
crowds try to get into the U.S.Embassy and go
to helipad on roof from where part of the
evacuation is being made.NOTE civilian clad
man with pistol pointed at the crowd.(APRADIO

Photograph 6   The fall of Saigon

References

Berry, B. J. L. and Garrison, W. (1958) 'Functional bases of the central place hierarchy', *Economic Geography*, **34**, 145–54.

Bradford, M. G. and Kent, A. (1977), *Human Geography*, Oxford University Press, Oxford.

Bunge, W. W. (1962), *Theoretical Geography*, Gleerup, Lund.

Carter, H. (1980), *The Study of Urban Geography*, 3rd edn. Arnold, London.

Davies, P. (1974), *Data Description and Presentation*, OUP, Oxford.

Davies, R. L. (1976), *Marketing Geography*, RPA Books, Northumberland.

Donnison, D. and Soto, P. (1980), *The Good City*, Heinemann, London.

Drewett, R., Goddard, J. B. and Spence, N. (1975), 'What's happening to British cities?', *Town and Country Planning*, **43** (12), 523–30.

Everson, J. A. and Fitzgerald, B. P. 1969, *Settlement Patterns*, Longman, London.

Haggett, P. (1979), *Geography – a modern synthesis*, McGraw-Hill, New York.

Hall, P. G. (1974), 'The new political geography', Institute of British Geographers. *Transactions* **63**, 48–52.

Hall, P. G. (1975), *Urban and Regional Planning*, Penguin, Harmondsworth.

Hall, P. G. (ed.) (1979), *The Penguin World Atlas*, Penguin, Harmondsworth.

Hall, P. G. and Hay, D. (1980), *Growth Centres in Europe*, Heinemann, London.

Lambert, D. M. (1981), 'Drawing boundaries around a conurbation', in Walford, R. (ed.) *Signposts in Geographical Education*, Longman, Harlow.

McCullagh, P. (1974), *Data use and interpretation*, OUP, Oxford.

Newton, K. (1981), 'Central Places and Urban Services', in Newton, K. (ed.) *Urban Political Economy*, Frances Pinter, London.

Richardson, H. W. (1973), *The Economics of City Size*, Saxon House, Farnborough.

Robson, B. T. (1973), *Urban Growth: an approach*, Methuen, London.

Robson, B. T. (1979), 'Housing, empiricism and the state', in Herbert, D. T. and Smith, D. M. (eds) *Social Problems and the City*, Oxford University Press, Oxford.

Shannon, G. and Dever, G. E. A. (1974), *Health-Care Delivery*, McGraw-Hill, New York.

Smailes, A. E. (1971), 'Urban Systems', Institute of British Geographers, *Transactions* **53**, 1–14.

Vance, J. E. (1970), *The Merchant's World*, Prentice-Hall, Englewood Cliffs, New Jersey.

Zipf, G. (1949), *Human Behaviour and the Principle of Least Effort*, Reading, Massachusetts.